An OPUS book

Existentialism

MARY WARNOCK

Existentialism

Oxford New York

OXFORD UNIVERSITY PRESS

Oxford University Press, Walton Street, Oxford OX2 6DP

Oxford New York
Athens Auckland Bangkok Bombay
Calcutta Cape Town Dar es Salaam Delhi
Florence Hong Kong Istanbul Karachi
Kuala Lumpur Madras Madrid Melbourne
Mexico City Nairobi Paris Singapore
Taipei Tokyo Toronto

and associated companies in
Berlin Ibadan

Oxford is a trade mark of Oxford University Press

British Library Cataloguing in Publication Data
Data available

ISBN 0-19-888052-9

10 9

Printed in Great Britain by
Biddles Ltd
Guildford and King's Lynn

Contents

Acknowledgements

Acknowledgements are due to those who have kindly given permission for the quotation in this book of copyright material from Søren Kierkegaard, *Concluding Unscientific Postscript*, translated by David F. Swenson and Walter Lowrie for the American Scandinavian Foundation (Copyright, 1941, by Princeton University Press); from Maurice Merleau-Ponty, *The Phenomenology of Perception*, translated by Colin Smith (Routledge & Kegan Paul, Ltd., London; and Humanities Press, Inc., New York): from translations of Jean-Paul Sartre, *Being and Nothingness*, previously published in the present author's Hutchinson University Library volume, *The Philosophy of Sartre* (Hutchinson & Co. (Publishers) Ltd.). Permission to publish previously unpublished translations from *Being and Nothingness* (Editions Gallimard) has been granted by Methuen & Co. Ltd., London, and the Philosophical Library Inc., New York.

1

Ethical Origins:
Søren Kierkegaard; Friedrich Nietzsche

'EXISTENTIALISM', like 'Rationalism' or 'Empiricism', is a label
that may mislead the unwary. It does not designate a system or a
school; there are some philosophers who might be described as
Existentialists but who would reject the title; others who might
be surprised to be so described. But in philosophy, as in the arts,
boundary disputes are not to be avoided, but are not really very
important. We may be content to use the term 'Existentialism'
to cover a kind of philosophical activity which flourished on the
Continent especially in the 1940s and 1950s, which can be shown
to have certain common interests, common ancestry and common
presuppositions, and which is now sufficiently clearly a matter
of history to make a general survey worth undertaking. This will
have to do as a starting point.

Broadly speaking, we can say that the common interest which
unites Existentialist philosophers is the interest in human freedom.
They are all of them interested in the world considered as the
environment of man, who is treated as a unique object of attention,
because of his power to choose his own courses of action. What
his freedom of choice amounts to and how it is to be described
. . . these are topics of central concern to all Existentialists. But
many philosophers have been concerned with human freedom,
with the 'problem of the freedom of the will', who have not been
Existentialists. So, it is necessary to add that for Existentialists,
uniquely, the problem of freedom is in a sense a practical problem.
They aim, above all, to show people *that they are free*, to open
their eyes to something which has always been true, but which for
one reason or another may not always have been recognized,

namely that men are free to choose, not only what to do on a specific occasion, but what to value and how to live. The readers of Existentialist philosophy are being asked, not merely to consider the nature of human freedom, but to *experience* freedom, and to practise it. In this respect the Existentialists are like Spinoza, who, having shown what man's place in the universe is, has shown thereby a new way to look at human emotions and human understanding. But it is Spinoza inverted that we are here considering; for whereas he wanted us to learn that freedom of the will was an illusion, based upon ignorance of causes, the Existentialist characteristically wants us to learn that the freedom which we experience, the *sense* of freedom which we have, is justified; and moreover that, in some sense, causation is an illusion. This, then, emerges as the second characteristic concern of Existentialists: to convert their readers, to get them to accept that up to now they have been deluded, but can now see things in a new light. This is the missionary spirit of Existentialism, which will appear in many guises, but whose tone is unmistakable. Any philosopher presumably wishes his readers to accept what he says as true or plausible, as a satisfactory explanation of phenomena in the world, or as a satisfactory way to classify them; but Existentialists want more than this. They want the facts about human freedom, as they conceive them, to be not merely accepted, but absorbed by each person for himself, so that when he has absorbed them, his whole view of his life will be different. Someone in the process of reading and understanding an Existentialist philosopher ought to be in the grip of a mood which actually transforms his way of seeing the world and his place in it. As a religious conversion might transform one's view, or as a metaphysical theory might transform it, by making one see oneself in relation to other people or the universe differently, as Proust's actual view of occurrences was transformed by a Bergsonian theory of time—so Existentialists hope to be not merely intellectually, but emotionally and practically, innovators. Thus, because Existentialism is concerned with man's freedom, and because it aims to change its readers, to free them from illusion and to convert them, it follows that it has always been thought of, with justice, as a committed and practical philosophy. I hope to show more clearly later the way in which these practical aspects of Existentialism arise, and how they are founded on a theoretical connection between cognition and volition, between knowing and doing. It is enough for the time being to note the missionary and practical aim of Existentialism, and to suggest that part of its attraction, especially to people brought up on the austerities of Anglo-Saxon philosophy, has been precisely this insistence that mere intellectual understanding is not enough.

So much for the common interests. The common ancestry of Existentialism must be divided into two parts. First, there is that tradition which is the main subject of this chapter, the ethical tradition whose emphasis was upon man as the possessor of a will, man as a voluntary agent. This ethical tradition can itself be divided, though perhaps not very significantly, into that part which is theological and that which is secular. Under these headings I mean to discuss first Kierkegaard and then Nietzsche.

The second element in the common Existentialist ancestry is completely different from, and in many ways diametrically opposed to, ethical voluntarism. It is the phenomenology of Husserl. The marriage of these two elements is essential to Existentialism, and I do not count as an Existentialist philosopher anyone who cannot prove this particular parentage. Thus many non-philosophical writers who have been influenced by Kierkegaard or by Nietzsche, and who have written 'Existentialist' novels, plays, diaries or essays, will not be considered in the chapters that follow, and I think there is reason in this. For Existentialism, as here considered, is a kind of philosophy, and though, as we have seen, it is largely practical in its intentions, and though it has had more impact upon literature than possibly any other kind of philosophy, yet there is a point in treating it as philosophy in some fairly strict sense, in order, among other things, to compare it with other kinds of philosophy. Without, therefore, being so rash as to attempt a definition of philosophy, it nevertheless seems possible to distinguish philosophical from non-philosophical Existentialism. The non-philosophical Existentialist will share the common interests of his philosophical cousin, but he will not share a method. This is not just a matter of what form he chooses to write in, but rather of whether or not he is attempting a *systematic* account of man's connection with the world. The *method* of philosophical Existentialism could not have come into being without Husserl's phenomenology. We shall therefore consider Husserl in the next chapter, before going on to the Existentialists themselves. But first of all we will turn to the ethical ancestry.

Very broad classifications and distinctions in ethical theory are probably not very illuminating, though it is sometimes amusing to make them; but just occasionally a philosopher stands out as a genuine innovator, so that it seems that after his time all other philosophers must in some sense be for him or against him. Kant was such a figure in the history of ethical theory. Kant started from the conviction that people know that they are subject to a moral law, and know that they sometimes have to decide what they are going to do, and then do it. His theory begins and ends with the thought of a human *agent*, faced with a decision, and actually bringing his will to bear on the world, freely. I do not of course want to suggest that Kant actually invented the idea of practical reason; many other philosophers, including Aristotle, had been concerned with the question of how reasons for acting bring a man finally to act. What is new in Kant is the way in which, knowing exactly that this is what he is doing, he derives the whole concept of the morally good (and bad) from the concept of the agent's will.

Things in the world may be pleasant or unpleasant, desirable or undesirable, just as they may be sweet or sour, hard or soft. But they cannot be morally good or bad. Moral value is something which springs into being only when there is an actual human agent deciding what to do, and doing it. No amount of description of the world, or of human tastes or tendencies, could bring into being any idea of value; this could be introduced only at the moment when one introduced into the description the free will of an agent. What this agent actually achieves in his attempt to act on the world is quite irrelevant to the value introduced by his act of will. Unless one knew how a man chose, what exactly he willed to bring about, then no amount of observing what he *did* would entitle one to assign a value to the change that he actually brought about. There is, therefore, on this theory, an immense gap between human beings and all other beings in the world. For only human beings are dynamic; only they can voluntarily bring about changes in the world, and bring them about for a particular reason. Everything in the world except an act of will can, according to Kant, be described in causal terms; and this is the same as to say that nothing has any value except the act of will, which brings values into existence.

Now Kant himself believed that, although human beings brought value into the world in that they, and only they, could choose to act, yet there were absolute laws according to which they must act if their acts were to be morally good. Indeed this belief in absolute law was his starting point; it was the phenomenon to be explained. He believed that, if one reflects, one just knows that one is subject to absolute laws. But his explanation of this phenomenon was new. The absolute nature of the moral law had no external source. It derived from the will itself, which was both its subject and its ultimate authority. For Kant, the voice of reason was identical with the voice of the good will; and therefore just as, if one person reasons logically from a given set of premises, and another person goes through the same argument, their conclusions will be identical, so, if two people, faced with the same situation, both exercise their will rationally, they will both do the same thing. The moral law is both generated by the agent, and absolute and objectively binding upon everyone, because it is the law of reason.

Such is Kant's theory; but it is easy to see how an ethical theory could develop out of Kant's which, while insisting, as his did, that values are created only by an agent choosing to act in the world, might yet abandon the view that this will must, to be good, be *rational*, and legislate universally. The central belief of ethical voluntarism is the Kantian belief that human beings are totally different from all other beings in the universe by reason of their will, the existence of which is the source of all value. Voluntarists would agree with Kant in rejecting all kinds of Utilitarianism, on the grounds that, although it may be true on the whole that good acts maximize happiness, it is not true that their goodness *derives from* their maximization of happiness. There may be other things in the world, like nice weather, which maximize happiness and are not good because they were not intended to do so. Only an act of will can have value. There is no value in things which merely happen, through nobody's choice.

Now there is no possibility of acts of will themselves being common to more than one person. I cannot exercise your will or make your decision, any more than I can, literally, speak with your voice or walk with your legs. You may advise me or command me, but in the end, even if I do what you tell me, or what anyone would have done, I do it myself. My acts are my own. So it is possible that the value of my act of will may attach to it as mine, whereas if you had done the same thing there would have been no value in your act of will. F. H. Bradley, who was completely in the voluntarist tradition deriving ultimately from Kant, actually thought it a distinguishing mark of a moral, as opposed to an aesthetic, act that it *made a difference who performed it*. That an act was mine is part of its value or disvalue; whereas there is a sense in which, if a good poem has been written, it exists as a good object whoever wrote it. This was a part of what Bradley meant by the saying that self-realization was the goal of the moral act. There is no necessary presupposition that what would be a realization of one self would be a realization of another.

To return at last to Existentialism, and to the two philosophers whose work is the ethical origin of Existentialism, Kierkegaard and Nietzsche: both of them in different ways abandon the rational and universal standard of morality, while insisting, with Kant, on the creative aspect of the will, that is, on the view that only acts of will create anything which can be valued, either high or low.

Søren Kierkegaard was born in 1813, and died in 1855. It is impossible to understand his work without understanding a little of his life. As a young child, he was very much affected by the religion of his father, which was sombre and gloomy, and conducive to the deepest sense of guilt and sin. Later, as a young man, he threw off this influence as far as he could, and, for a time, believed himself to have escaped entirely. He gave up his time to learning as much as he could of the world and to enjoying himself. In 1836, he underwent a kind of moral conversion, and for a time lived his life in accordance with strict and universalizable moral principles. Then, in 1838, he was converted to Christianity. Doubtless this tidy chronicle of affairs is misleading; but the interest of it is how Kierkegaard himself saw his life. Looking back on it, he sharply distinguished the stages through which he passed. His first emancipated years were called by him the Aesthetic Stage. At this time he had seemed to himself to enjoy freedom, but this freedom turned out to be illusory. The higher stage to which he next passed was also ultimately based upon an illusion: not, this time, the illusion of freedom, for in the ethical stage of his life he felt himself bound by laws of universal and absolute validity. The illusion was of 'humanism'; for the ethical laws which were the framework of his life had no transcendental backing, but were derived from human requirements, and fixed, social, standards. Being converted from this stage to Christianity, he threw off the humanistic illusion, and finally adopted the standpoint of faith.

Kierkegaard came to see these three stages in his own life as general stages in the development of human beings, who may live at any one of the stages for the whole of their lives, or may move from the lower to the higher. But each move to a higher stage must be a move which the individual man himself *decides* to make. It is futile just to tell someone to become ethical, or to adopt the standpoint of faith; and arguments to show that a man would be better-off or happier if he moved, or that society demands it of him, are all insufficient to make a man change his way of life. The conversion must be genuine. The man converted must suddenly come to see that what he had taken for reality before was all the time illusion. Like the prisoners in Plato's cave, he must face about, and recognize the shadows on the wall for what they are. To adopt a new belief is not merely to adopt a set of propositions which intellectually seem more plausible or more defensible; for Kierkegaard, a belief must be accepted as something true *for* the individual, as something by which he is prepared to live, and to which he has a non-rational commitment.

Here we can see for the first time what has already been mentioned as a characteristic of all Existentialist writing, the desire to change one's readers, to free them from their past illusions, and make them not only think, but even live differently. Kierkegaard himself takes Socrates as his model, who had no further aim than to make the Sophists, and those who were taught by them, realize that the Sophists' learning was delusive. Neither in the teaching of Socrates nor in that of Kierkegaard is there any distinction to be drawn between intellectual and moral error. To be subject to illusion is to be in a benighted state; and when one recognizes illusion for what it is one hates it, and loves the light. Seeing the truth is seeing the light which illuminates one's own personal path. One person can help another, no doubt, as Socrates helped his pupils. But when Socrates claimed to know nothing, that is to have *nothing* to teach in the way that the Sophists taught, he was suggesting that conversion is not an intellectual but an emotional and ethical event in a man's life.

The illusion from which Kierkegaard himself, above all, wanted to free people was the illusion of *objectivity*. This was the illusion most likely not only in fact to dominate their thought, but actually to be welcomed by them as enlightenment and progress. He says that we have lost the capacity for subjectivity, and it is the task of philosophy to rediscover it for us.

We must consider what Kierkegaard means by 'objectivity' and 'subjectivity'. Objectivity shows itself in the tendency to accept rules governing both behaviour and thought. Any subject-matter which is bound by rules of evidence, or which can be taught in the class-room, is in the grip of objectivity. History is objective if it is thought of as something within which the true and the false can be definitely, once for all, sorted out and distinguished; it is objective if some propositions are rejected on the basis of a general rule, either of what counts as evidence, or of what can be accepted as plausible human behaviour. Sociology and psychology would be totally objective studies, and therefore unacceptable in principle, because they attempt to generalize, predict or explain the behaviour of human groups or individuals according to scientific laws. Morality is objective as soon as it is encapsulated in a code or set of rules, which can be passed on from teacher to pupil.

There are many people who can live their whole lives, as Kierkegaard lived a short part of his, under the domination of objectivity, bound by a set of moral principles which could be written down and petrified as a code. The objective tendency is, he says, that which 'proposes to make everyone an observer, and in its maxims to transform him into so objective an observer that he becomes almost a ghost'. And of the ethical stage of life he says: 'That the individual must become an observer is the ethical answer to the problem of life.' If one becomes an observer, one may treat the whole of life in one of two ways, either as history or as natural science. An observer perpetually raises the question 'by what natural law is human behaviour determined?' and he is obliged to raise the same question about his own behaviour. He asks 'What role am I playing?' or 'How am I to be described?' and thus the spontaneity and inwardness of his life is lost.

The myth which Kierkegaard aims to destroy is the scientific myth that everything is causally determined, and that therefore in principle a complete and objectively true account of the behaviour of everything could be provided, if only we took trouble and observed enough. This scientific myth could dominate not only a man's ethical but also his religious life, and it is for this domination that Kierkegaard saves his most violent hostility.

> An objective acceptance of Christianity (sit venia verbo) is paganism or thoughtlessness . . . Christianity protests against every form of objectivity; it desires that the subject should be infinitely concerned about himself. It is with subjectivity that Christianity is concerned, and it is only in subjectivity that its truth exists, if it exists at all. Objectively, Christianity has absolutely no existence. If the truth happens to be only in a single subject it exists in him alone; and there is greater Christian joy in heaven over this one individual than over universal history or the system.[1]

Objectivity, then, is the acceptance of the role of the observer, who adopts or discovers general laws. But it is not easy to discard objectivity. Subjectivity, paradoxical as it may seem, is hard to achieve. For though in fact each of us is an individual, and we are therefore capable of thinking our own thoughts and living our lives in inwardness, that is spontaneously, and capable of choosing for ourselves what to do, yet it is far easier for us to identify ourselves with a group or a sect and think their thoughts and accept their standards. Intellectually we are prone, the more we know, more and more to become impersonal, and to think of ourselves as contributing absolutely to some great corpus of human knowledge in general. In such ways as these, the individual loses himself in the mass, and ceases to recognize that 'the knower is an existing individual'.

There are three essential characteristics of subjective knowledge. First, it cannot be passed on from one person to the next, nor added to by different researchers. It cannot be taught in the classroom. Second, what is known subjectively always has the nature of a paradox. Therefore subjective knowledge is identical with faith. For faith alone, and not reason, can induce us to accept paradox. Faith is not an intellectual, but an emotional attribute. Kierkegaard says: 'Christianity wishes to intensify passion to the highest pitch; but passion is subjectivity, and does not exist objectively.'[2] Third, subjective knowledge is concrete, not abstract. This is because it must necessarily be related to the actual concrete

---

[1] *Concluding Unscientific Postscript*, trans. D. F. Swenson and W. Lowrie (Princeton U.P., Princeton, N.J., 1941), p. 116.
[2] op. cit., p. 117.

existence of a living individual. The contrast between objective and subjective truth is brought out in the following passage:

When the question of truth is raised in an objective manner, reflection is directed objectively to the truth as an object to which the knower is related. Reflection is not focussed on the relationship, however, but upon the question whether it is the truth to which the knower is related. If only the object to which he is related is the truth, the subject is accounted to be in the truth. When the question of truth is raised subjectively, reflection is directed subjectively to the nature of the individual's relationship; if only the mode of this relationship is in the truth, the individual is in the truth, even if he should happen to be thus related to what is not true.[1]

Thus it appears that *what* a man believes is less important than *the manner in which* he believes it; as long as he realizes his own status as the concrete individual thinker of a thought, which he *need not* think but does think for himself, then whether the thought is, objectively speaking, true does not matter. The individual is 'in the truth'. Again, Kierkegaard says:

When subjectivity, inwardness, is the truth, the truth becomes objectively a paradox; and the fact that the truth is objectively a paradox shows in its turn that subjectivity is the truth. For the objective situation (of entertaining a paradoxical thought) is repellent, and the expression for the objective repulsion constitutes the tension and the measure of the corresponding inwardness. The paradoxical character of the truth is its objective uncertainty. This uncertainty is the expression for the passionate inwardness, and this passion is precisely the truth. The eternal and essential truth, the truth which has an essential relationship to an existing individual because it pertains essentially to existence, is a paradox. But the eternal essential truth is by no means in itself a paradox; but it becomes paradoxical by virtue of its relationship to an existing individual.[2]

This paradoxical thought in relation to a thinker is concrete thought. It is always a struggle to think in concrete terms, because there is necessarily a gap between thought and that of which it is a thought. 'What is abstract thought?' Kierkegaard asks.

It is thought without a thinker. Abstract thought ignores everything except the thought, and only the thought is, and is in its own medium. Existence is not devoid of thought, but in existence thought is in a foreign medium. What can it then mean to ask in the language of

[1] op. cit., p. 178.   [2] op. cit., p. 183.

abstraction about reality in the sense of existence, seeing that abstract thought abstracts precisely from existence? What is concrete thought? It is thought with a relation to a thinker, and to a definite particular something which is thought, existence giving to the thinker thought, time and place.[1]

Of Socrates it was the case that his inwardness was his whole life, his method of philosophical enquiry, his asking of questions and shattering of accepted presuppositions and pretensions to knowledge. Objectively, the result of the Socratic enquiry was always to produce confusion and bewilderment. But subjectively, it produced the truth. The Socratic ignorance arose from Socrates' awareness of himself as an individual, thinking alone, without the support of the rules or laws of the Sophists' methods. He thought of himself as an existing concrete individual, set down in the world, and raising questions about the world. This ignorance is the precursor of the *absurd*, the irrational and inexplicable *fact* that an individual lives in the world he does live in. The absurd is that part of a man's situation which is intractable to generalizations or system-making. It is the brute fact that he exists as a concrete thing in the world. To accept the absurd is to accept a paradox, and for this one needs faith.

In the case of Christianity, the easy way out is once more to think of Christian doctrine as objective truth, as something which can be made rational, and can be learned and taught in dogma. To objectify Christianity is immediately to render it trivial. The central paradox of Christianity is the Incarnation, in which God who 'does not think but creates, who does not exist but is eternally' actually came into existence in a particular place and at a particular time. This paradox, which is the beginning and end of absurdity, cannot be made rationally, objectively acceptable, but can be known only subjectively. A Christianity which is supposed to be objectively true, let alone acceptable to science, is a contradiction. But most of the time people find it hard to bear the thought of their own individuality, their own responsibility for their thoughts. They suffer from 'absentmindedness'. Hence, to turn a man round so that he sees himself as a concrete individual is a conversion. It is far easier for him to conceal this fact from himself. He will prefer to accept an explanation of the paradox rather than the paradox itself.

[1] op. cit., p. 296.

An explanation of the paradox makes it clear what the paradox is, removing any obscurity remaining; a correction takes the paradox away, and makes it clear that there is no paradox. But if the paradox arises from putting the eternal and an existing particular human being into relation with one another, when the speculative explanation takes the paradox away, does the explanation also take existence away from the existing individual? And when the existing individual . . . has been brought to the point where it seems to him as nearly as possible that he does not exist, what is he then? Why then he is absent-minded. . . . Thus everything is in order. The explanation is that the paradox is the paradox only to a certain degree, and it is quite in order that such an explanation should be valid for an existing individual who is an existing individual only to a certain degree, since he forgets it every other moment. Such an existing individual is precisely a person who suffers from absentmindedness.[1]

These passages from Kierkegaard may be enough to show the sense in which he is the parent of Existentialism. Subjectivity and concreteness of truth are together the light. Anyone who is committed to science, or to rule-governed morality, is benighted, and needs to be rescued from his state of darkness.

A man who is converted is shown that he is free. In the first place he is free to choose whether to move from one stage of enlightenment to another. This is the primary exercise of freedom, and if men were not free they could not be enlightened, since accepting the true state of affairs is an act of a concrete individual, which cannot be done on his behalf by anyone but himself. If I try to accept the truth on your behalf, then I have misunderstood the nature of the truth. The truth exists for you and it exists for me, but each of us must grasp it for himself. This is what 'inwardness' amounts to.

Secondly, men are free because they are able to think for themselves, and need not have recourse to laws, to rules, nor to the standards of history and science. This freedom is identical with isolation. If one is entirely alone on a desert island then, though one may not be free in all senses of the word, there is yet an important sense in which one is free. For the whole responsibility of deciding how to live rests with oneself. All the props of civilization, the supports of morality, the law, and institutionalized religion and learning, have been removed. It is in this desert island sense

[1] op. cit., p. 196.

that Kierkegaard's man of faith is free. He is self-governing. And more than that, he is creative. Nothing on his island is valuable unless he makes it so. If he comes trailing relics of accepted values, codes, or rules behind him, then he is not a moral man. His morality lies precisely in the fact that he is discovering the truth for himself, in inwardness.

But all the same, his inwardness, his faith and subjectivity, do lead him to be aware of something other than himself, however self-aware they also make him. The stage of faith is the stage of awareness of the transcendental, of some aspect of life which is different from the concrete particular existing objects, though related to them through himself. In religious thought, a man's isolation can never be absolute. Kierkegaard would not claim that man could *know* God, or His will. To claim this would at once be to reduce God to the compass of the human understanding, or, probably, to reintroduce theology, and general ethical values. It would be, once again, to 'objectify' Christianity. But all the same, faith, in grasping the paradox of Christianity, can comfort its possessor. '*Non vos relinquam orphanos*' remains a promise to the faithful, even if they cannot, and must not, analyse its content.

The total independence and isolation of free man is found for the first time in Nietzsche. Although both Kierkegaard and Nietzsche have been referred to as the ethical ancestors of Existentialism, ultimately the moral philosophy of both of them stems from a theory of truth. Ethics is an offshoot, and perhaps not the most important offshoot, of a far more general philosophy. Like Kierkegaard, Nietzsche regarded 'objectivity' as the main enemy of understanding. For him objectivity meant the myth that there are hard, identifiable facts in the world, about which such hard, definite statements can be made that they can, with sufficient care, be made to fit or correspond to the facts. Against this view he argued that all the concepts which we employ in describing the world and predicting its behaviour are imposed upon it by ourselves. We have a choice about what view of the world to adopt.

There is a kind of Kantian flavour about the proposition that we make the world conform to our concepts, but Nietzsche's position is both vaguer and more radical than Kant's Copernican Revolution. For Nietzsche held that there is no sharp line to be drawn between describing and evaluating. Even in the most apparently objective and scientific description of phenomena there enters an element of choice in the classification, and of preference or rejection. 'Our very sense perceptions', he says, 'are altogether permeated with valuations (useful or harmful, hence acceptable or unacceptable)', and 'even the individual colours express a value for us. Even insects react differently to different colours, one preferring this, another that.' People have been unwilling to face the fact that there is no possibility of building up an objective corpus of scientific knowledge which would be true for all time, and therefore they have canonized some of their myths and prejudices and named them 'truth'.

We select the concepts which we use for describing and making statements about the world ultimately to suit our own ends. Valuation, as we have seen, enters even our most everyday descriptions, depending upon what we like or dislike, or upon what we find harmful or helpful to our purposes. Fundamentally, human beings wish to dominate and manipulate the world, to manage their environment. This is necessarily true for creatures who are characterized above all by the power to act, that is, deliberately to change their situation. If men had no will they would not be men; but, having a will, they inevitably seek to change the world to suit them. 'Our cognitive apparatus is an abstracting and falsifying mechanism', Nietzsche wrote, 'directed not towards knowledge, but towards mastery and possession.' Even the longing which people feel for absolute objective certainty is born of the desire to master and control the world, for it is simply the desire for security, 'the longing for a handle or support, and instinct of weakness, which even if it does not create religions, metaphysics, creeds of every sort, nevertheless conserves them'.

Absolute objective truth, then, is an illusion. The Cartesian search for certainty was the outcome of fear. It was also connected with what Nietzsche believed to be a fundamental error in the concept of a human being. For Descartes's man was composed of two elements, the mind and the body. *Res cogitans* was completely and totally distinct from *Res extensa*, two different substances. The mind lodged in the body, and, peering out from it, perceived the world dimly through the medium of the senses. But genuine certainty came from the mind's own operations within itself. The greatest difficulty, for Descartes, was to explain how the mind co-operated with the body, how perception and action ever occurred. For Nietzsche there was no such problem. The 'ghost in the machine' was abolished, and the concept of man was unified, so that cognition and action were not two separate functions, but were part of the same operation, the operation of the will.

The pre-eminence of the will as the characteristic feature of man, which in Kant had had relevance only in ethics, in Nietzsche become equally important, whatever activity of man one is considering. The will is not a cause of action, for one cannot consider the will and the act as sufficiently separated for a causal relation between them to be intelligible. One should not think of the will as an identifiable active force, but simply as *the man*. Introspection is not more likely to give us certain truths than is perception of the outside world. 'The "apparent inner world" is manipulated with just the same forms and procedures as "the external world". We never hit upon "facts".' Our whole life, cognitive, ethical, practical and creative, is the concern of our will, which just is the power to change things. The will to power is identical with the will to live. If we are alive and conscious then we must plan and aim to master our world. We experience it as a world-to-be-mastered.

We shall see later how this anti-Cartesian account of our actual experience of the world becomes the centre of Existentialist thought. We shall, moreover, see the very same anti-Cartesianism in the different setting of Husserl's phenomenology. Anti-Cartesianism, indeed, becomes the characteristic of Existentialist thought which is inherited from both of its ancestors. One must at no time be deceived by the pious words uttered by Sartre and Merleau-Ponty about Descartes. There is no more determining factor in their thought than the rejection of Cartesian dualism.

The will to power is essentially practical, and from it arises, naturally, not only our decisions as to the classification and description of the world, but also our decisions as to behaviour. Since there is no such thing, in Nietzsche's view, as absolute objective truth in science, there is plainly none in the field of morality either. Evaluation, the designating things good or bad, is nothing to do with knowing truths; it is itself a form of activity, and forms part of all activity. Throughout his work, Nietzsche insists that his task is to distinguish moralists and philosophers of morals from scientists. Scientists themselves are wrong to think that they are actually discovering hard objective facts about the world, but moralists would be still more wrong to think so of themselves.

Their role is to *make* standards, not to find them, 'as though values were inherent in things, so that all we had to do was keep our hold on them'. Evaluative judgements are 'active'. Moralists must legislate, but even their legislation cannot be expected to be absolute or to have general application, for if it did, it would generate judgements of absolute values, which cannot exist. The world lies open to interpretation; value is nothing but our interpretation of phenomena, and we may interpret them as we wish.

Thus Nietzsche's moral philosophy is on the one hand a total rejection of ethical naturalism. The naturalistic philosopher holds that ethical values derive from certain observable features of the world, which human beings are all of them bound to evaluate in a particular way. The strongest case for naturalism has always been put by Utilitarians of one kind or another, for they hold that men inevitably seek pleasure and avoid pain, and that therefore they value highly and call good anything which leads to pleasure, and they regard as bad anything which leads to pain. Since it is supposed by Utilitarians to be an observable fact that some things are pleasurable and others painful, it follows that one can establish laws of good behaviour which will have universal application, and which can be tested empirically, to see if they do indeed produce behaviour which is good. For a Utilitarian it should always be possible to answer for certain the question whether or not a particular kind of behaviour is good.

On the other hand, Nietzsche was equally opposed to ethical institutionism, or any other kind of theory which held that ethical values were fixed, stable and *there* to be discovered, whether by pure reason, by intuition, or by revelation. The essential truth, as he saw it, was that men choose their own values; just as in describing the world they choose those categories of descriptions which seem most useful, which enable them to manipulate the world best, so, still more manifestly, they exercise their will to power in praising and admiring those features of the world which help them to dominate and master their environment.

Nietzsche treats the relativity and variation of moralities as a special case of the relativity of all attitudes to the world. But he held, notoriously, that from the anthropological standpoint one could classify all moralities under one of two heads. They were either master or slave moralities. In each case it could be shown that the qualities admired as virtues—kindness, pity, charity by the slaves, and pride, power, courage by the masters—were useful for the survival of the kind of persons who adopted such a morality. But in every case, a man could simply decide to value something else, whatever happened to be the typical values of his society.

At this point we should notice again something like the missionary spirit which was characteristic of Kierkegaard. Nietzsche, like Kierkegaard, and like all true Existentialist philosophers, wished to free people from the shackles of illusion. The illusion in this case is, of course, that of the immutability of first scientific, and then moral law. Most people simply accept without question the morality of their society, and feel themselves bound by it. Nietzsche tells them that they are not really bound; they have, being human, the will which enables them to adopt some different laws for themselves.

There is no doubt that Nietzsche's 'transvaluation of values' is really nothing but a new understanding of what evaluation is, a new way of looking at the phenomenon of morality in general. But sometimes his language would suggest that he is making a different point, namely that there ought to be no moral values at all. This is a familiar difficulty. Any philosopher who aims to give a new account of a particular phenomenon, and to argue that this phenomenon has been wrongly understood up to his time, is liable to get carried away, and to appear to be debunking the phenomenon itself rather than the accepted explanation of it. For example, Hume set out to give a new account of our belief in the continued and independent existence of the outside world, and sought to analyse the belief in it, which we undoubtedly have, in terms of the faculty of imagination, which allows us to fill up gaps in our actual sensory experience of the world. But often his language suggests, not that he is explaining a belief which we all hold quite justifiably, but that he is telling us that we ought not to hold the belief, that it is a belief in something 'feigned' or 'fictitious'. Similarly in *Language, Truth and Logic*, A. J. Ayer, who was really distinguishing evaluative from fact-stating discourse in respect of verifiability, and was giving an emotive analysis of evaluative judgements, was led into using terms to describe such judgements which suggested that no sane person ought to make them. In rather the same way, Nietzsche frequently attacks morality as such, and the established morality in particular. In some of his writings it is easy to interpret him as preaching a doctrine of immorality, or cruelty, violence and self-interest.

But in fact, his message has two parts. The first is that men *can* choose a different set of values; they *need not* be bound by conventional morality, which has no special status. The second is that they ought to choose a different set of values. There is no doubt that he says both these things. But the first is as important as the second, and it is the first which arises directly out of his general theory of a man's position as a creature with a will, who can will to change his world. The difficulty in reading Nietzsche is that the rhetoric associated with the second part of his message spills over and sometimes obscures the first part. In fact what we are being asked to do is to re-examine the status and justifiability of our moral beliefs.

Nietzsche agreed with Kant that morality was essentially a matter of laws. It is the moral law which constrains a man to act in a manner which he would not choose if it were not for the law. Laws are the instruments of the will, through which the will imposes itself on the world. It is only through the creation of and conformity to laws that civilization has been able to advance at all. He writes: 'Every morality is, in opposition to *laisser aller*, a bit of tyranny against nature, even against reason' (*Beyond Good and Evil*); and, later in the same work, 'The remarkable fact is that whatever is of freedom, subtlety, daring, dance and firmness that is or ever was in the world, be it in thinking or ruling, in speaking or persuading, in art as in moral conduct, is made possible primarily by this "tyranny of arbitrary rules".' He sees clearly, that is to say, that morality is a kind of discipline; that what is admired morally, as opposed to any other way, is that which is not easy or natural, in some sense, for man. Morality is a standard which it requires some effort to attain to.

Nietzsche, like Kant, is inclined perhaps to identify this disciplinary character of moralty with legislation. However, his concept of legislation is entirely different from Kant's, and is indeed full of difficulties and ambiguities. Kant believed that there could be no moral law which did not have universal applicability. Though each man exercised his freedom by legislating for himself, his will was morally good only if the law which he imposed upon himself were such as should also be imposed on every other rational creature. The moral agent does not, on Kant's view, think of himself as an individual, with particular wishes and needs of his own, but only as a member of a community of interlocking aims, a 'self-legislating member of the kingdom of ends'. Thus, just as when I employ a valid argument, it is a matter of no importance whose argument this is (for if my proof is valid, it is so whoever employs it), so, in the sphere of moral choice, if I reach the conclusion that a particular action would be right, then this conclusion would do for anyone in my position. It is totally immaterial who I am or what I may happen to want. If I am right for myself, then I am right for anyone else in the world who may seek my advice on this moral point. In making my decision, I am in effect legislating for the world. If I do not understand this, then I am making a random, and not a fully moral, act of will.

Nietzsche rejected the whole doctrine of the unversalizability of the moral law. For him, to legislate meant to legislate for oneself. He rightly argues that 'universalizing one's maxim' according to the Kantian formula is not a straightforward operation, since an evaluative element comes into the decision to describe one's act in a particular way. For example, if, when I have been asked an embarrassing question, I decide I ought to answer truthfully, because it is right to tell the truth, then I am supposed, by Kant, to be deciding that everyone ought to do the same in the same circumstances. But how do I know what is to count either as the 'same circumstances' or as 'doing the same'?

These are familiar arguments. From them Nietzsche concludes that though I may bind myself to tell the truth in this case, and though it is my legislating will that so binds me, the law my will creates is a law for me and me only. It may well be objected that a law made for myself alone is hardly a law; and it seems to me that this objection is unanswerable. Indeed Nietzsche himself, more happily, speaks not of laws but of ideals which an individual may hold up before himself and strive to attain. An ideal, scarcely less than a law, produces the kind of tension, the discipline, without which, as he clearly saw, there can be no morality. But it makes sense for an ideal, as it does not for a law, to constrain only that one person whose ideal it is. The ideal makes a claim upon me if it is my ideal. Nietzsche says that the claim is experienced not as 'Thou shalt' but as 'I will', and ultimately as 'I am', since it is in virtue of my own choices that I am what I am.

There is probably a further problem here, even if we adopt the word 'ideal' to characterize the standard which the individual will sets before itself in making choices. For it does not seem self-evident to what extent, if one has adopted an ideal of conduct oneself, one is entitled to attempt to impose this upon others. After all, it could be argued that if the ideal is one of *good* or *right* behaviour, then the universal element is re-introduced, and that if an ideal is a good one then it is good whoever adopts it. But it seems to me that Nietzsche is not to be blamed for not resolving this problem, which is, in practical life, exceedingly intractable.

There remains for him a further difficulty, or rather two related difficulties, which appear in different forms in the writings of Existentialist philosophers. First, he says that since moral evaluation, or, at the very least, evaluation of some sort, is inevitable for any creature endowed with a will, it follows that the one essential for the morally adult man is to create his own system of values and to reject the stock morality of his group. What is generally referred to as 'the moral code' is simply the system of evaluation accepted as inevitable and absolute by the unthinking, sheep-like majority of any society. The moral man must stand out from the herd. The question then arises, who can be moral? It is manifestly absurd to suggest that everyone can be outstanding. It is from this difficulty that the most notorious views of Nietzsche stem, the insistence upon the *élite* who shall impose their standards on the rest of their society.

Secondly, Nietzsche insists that 'To demand that our human interpretations and values should be general and perhaps even constitutive values belongs among the hereditary idiocies of human pride.' The moral man must, as we have seen, recognize that values are nothing in the world. They are what he creates by his power. 'The belief that the world as it should be really exists is a belief of those unproductive persons who do not wish to create the world as it should be. The will to truth is the impotence of the will to power.' The moral man must realize that his values are transitory, contingent, and not such as to be the subject of factual judgements. Yet this same moral man aims in all his perception and judgement to dominate his world, and to bring it within his power. This will undoubtedly mean sometimes making judgements as if they were actually true. If one wants, in the crudest way, to persuade some-one else that one course of action is preferable to another, it is of no use to qualify ones judgements, or hedge them about with provisos, or even to call attention to their subjectivity and muta-bility. Part of the manipulation of the world must be actually to make the world as one has described it; and this may well entail treating one's evaluative appraisals as if they were absolute. One can no more combine, for ever, saying 'This is good' with 'I may be wrong' than one can combine 'This is true' with 'I may be mistaken'. It seems that, though above all things Nietzsche despised the man who *unthinkingly* accepts moral opinions as if they were facts, yet he must have been prepared to accord the highest praise to the man who imposes his values on other people as though they were absolute, knowing what he is doing. We shall see that there is a parallel to these difficulties in Sartre's discussion of the man of bad faith. The man who unthinkingly accepts his condition, in-cluding the moral code which he lives by, as if it were inevitable, is in bad faith. But the man who knows that he need not live as he does, but nevertheless decides to abide by the traditional moral code, need not be in bad faith. The difficulty may be to tell the difference between the two men. The state of grace, both for Nietzsche and for Sartre, is the state of enlightenment. Realize that you are free, *et fac quod vis*.

Finally, we should notice that there are in Nietzsche a number of indications of a view of morality quite different from that of the free exercise of the will to power. Sometimes he writes as though there were no freedom involved in evaluation at all. For example, in the unpublished notes he wrote: 'In evaluation is expressed the condition of one's preservation and growth. All our sense organs and our senses are developed only in accordance with these conditions.' Moral activity, on this view, is simply an out-crop of biological and sociological necessity. The morality of a group could no more be changed than could its physique or the biochemical composition of its blood. This is ethical naturalism of an extreme kind, though different from the naturalism which Nietzsche attacked. But into this path we need not follow him since, on the whole, the Existentialists did not.

Perhaps it is true that what both Kierkegaard and Nietzsche elicit from us is an emotional response. For both are, as we have seen, seeking to convert and enlighten us, and free us from our shackles. Emotionally accepting their gospel is a matter of seeing ourselves in a new way, in 'inwardness'. If we believe what they say, our lives will be different. The two great concepts which will have freed us are those of the free will and of solitude. For each of us, if we enter this mood, the world is a place in which each by himself has the power to choose his own life from the foundations, to choose what he is to be, because he can choose what to value. But, since this is true of each of us, it follows that each must take the full responsibility for his choice, alone. The only obedience to cultivate is obedience to one's own ideal. We cannot even fall back on the comforting aim of seeking truth and following it, since truth is illusion, and what we have to seek is a paradox. It is from such proud, gloomy and grand converts that Existentialist heroes are born.

2
Edmund Husserl

IT would be fairly near the truth to say that Existentialism is a compound of emotional and intellectual factors to an equal degree. This composition, unusual for philosophy, is perhaps the secret of its success. It is also what makes it difficult to write about. To a certain extent one has to succumb to the emotional pressures before one can expound the philosophy with any plausibility. I hope to have suggested in the last chapter some of the emotional features of Existentialism, and some of their sources. I want now to turn to one of the intellectual sources, equally powerful, fruitful and obscure. The chief of these sources is German Phenomenology. Indeed, it has become increasingly difficult, as more work is done on phenomenology, and as Existentialism concurrently begins to take its place as part of philosophical history, to distinguish the one from the other. In this chapter I shall try to extract from the philosophy of Husserl those features which appear to have had the greatest influence on Existentialist writers.

We shall find that, just as in the work of Kierkegaard there were to be discovered certain salient characteristics which not only dominate Existentialism, but partially define the concept of Existentialism itself, so in Husserl there are characteristics and interests which in one form or another, reappear again and again, and without which a philosopher could hardly be classed an Existentialist. There is, however, an element of paradox in the connection between the two kinds of philosophy, and there can be no doubt that Husserl himself would therefore have turned away in disgust from the full-blown Existentialism of Sartre. For Husserl aimed at scientific exactitude. He believed that phenomenology was not only a philosophical but a scientific method. It is extremely doubtful, in fact, whether such a claim has any justification. But at least the spirit in which he undertook his work, being one of scientific detachment, was very far from the spirit of involvement in which Sartre aimed to find the *verité vécue* of human attributes. It is worth noting the paradox, in case Husserl's own philosophy, interesting and difficult in its own right, should somehow get swept into the turgid chaos of later Continental writing.

Phenomenology began with the work of Franz Brentano. In 1874 he published a book called *Psychology from an Empirical Point of View*[1] in which he outlined a programme of descriptive psychology, relying on the notion of intentionality. Husserl, as is well known, referred to this programme as the origin of phenomenology: 'His conversion of the scholastic concept of intentionality into a descriptive root-concept of psychology constitutes a great discovery, apart from which phenomenology could not have come into being at all.' Brentano had raised the question what was the essential difference between the objects of empirical psychology and the objects of other kinds of empirical science. What, that is to say, is the difference between the earth's crust studied by geologists, or the birds studied by ornithologists, and the objects such as thoughts, emotions, decisions, studied by psychologists? The phenomena with which psychologists are concerned are, he says, ideas: 'And I understand here by "idea" not that which is conceived but the act of conceiving. That is, the hearing of a tone, the seeing of a coloured object, or the thinking of a general idea.' He goes on to say:

Every psychological phenomenon is characterised by that which the scholastics of the Middle Ages have called intentional inherent existence of an object, and what we, although not entirely in unambiguous terms, would call the relationship to a content, the tendency towards an object (by which we do not mean a reality) or the immanent 'objectivity'. Each contains something as an object in itself, although not each in the same way. In the idea something is conceived, in the judgment something is recognised or discovered, in loving loved, in hating hated, in desiring desired, and so on. . . . No physical phenomenon shows anything like this intentional inexistence. And thus we can define psychical

---

[1] *Psychologie vom empirischen Standpunkt.*

phenomena by saying that they are such phenomena as contain objects in themselves by way of intention.[1]

As a matter of fact it seems that Brentano was not himself entirely happy about the scholastic terminology, and his preferred characterization of the psychical, which is the only one listed in the table of contents, is simply that of *reference to an object*: 'no hearing without something heard, no hoping without something hoped', and so on.

As we can see from the first passage quoted above, the difference between one kind of psychological phenomenon and another is to be drawn by the different quality of the relation of each to its object; and these different qualities can be detected by immediate experience, or inner perception. Descriptive psychology proceeds by the exercise of inner perception, by which we can detect the difference between, for example, hoping something and fearing something: by the examination of the act or event itself.

The fundamental kind of psychical phenomenon is the idea or representation—the first of the examples listed in the first quotation from Brentano above. Every psychical phenomenon is either itself a representation, or is based upon one. That this is so is itself a matter of immediate experience. For when we think of *thinking*, and then move on to think of, say, *loving*, we experience a break. Moreover, when we try to conceive of a creature who could love but not think or represent or have an idea, we realize that we cannot do so. Thus the fundamental distinctions and, besides that, the order of priority among psychological phenomena are settled by a kind of perception, an intuition which requires no further proof of its findings. This fact has, as we shall see, considerable importance, both in phenomenology, and in Existentialism itself.

This, then, is the great contribution of Brentano, that psychological acts are directed to an object. He was himself led into considerable ambiguity about the ontological status of these objects. In one sense, there is a contrast between the objects, if there are any, of physical acts (acts such as hitting or chopping) and those of psychical acts; for the object of a physical act, though it may seem other than it is, must have existence; while the object of a psychical act need not exist. I can desire an imaginary country

[1] op. cit., ed. O. Kraus, p. 125; trans. H. Spiegelberg in *The Phenomenological Movement* (Nijhoff, The Hague, 1965), vol. i, p. 39.

as well as a real one. But the imaginary country cannot seem other than it is, as an object of my thought and desire. Considered as a psychological object, it is as it *seems*. And so there is another sense in which psychological objects must necessarily exist, somehow or other, in order to serve as referents for psychological acts.

Some of Brentano's followers, and indeed Brentano himself, spent much time and ingenuity on the question of the existence of the objects of thought. Brentano was deeply opposed to the multiplication of entities, and was as determined to eliminate shadowy subsistent objects, such as golden mountains, or the present king of France, as was Russell himself, whose famous Theory of Descriptions was precisely designed to perform this elimination. Brentano insisted that in the description of an act of thought there could be only two items, the thinker and the real object. Where there was no real object thought of, then the situation of a man thinking of, say, a golden mountain must contain only one item, the man, but an item *modified* in a particular way. Moreover, he held that although there were no real entities called universals, yet we could describe the real world only in terms which had universal significance, and we could not experience anything which was not at least universalizable. In pursuing these arguments, he became more and more interested in the analysis of language, and into this area we cannot follow him. But it is worth noticing that towards the end of his life he had moved a good distance away from what we think of as phenomenology, a term which, in fact, he used only in passing.

There was a further difficulty for Brentano's theory which should be briefly noticed. It seemed that the definition of the psychic or mental, as that which referred necessarily to an object, would very much narrow the range of mental events. For, it was argued, there is a considerable number of mental phenomena—such as, especially, moods—which cannot be said to have an object. Therefore if the definition was to be strictly applied, they would have to count as physical, not mental events. Brentano did not accept this consequence, but found another way out of the difficulty. He said that there were two possible objects for any mental phenomenon, a primary object and a secondary object. The primary object was whatever it was that was *outside*, to which the phenomenon referred, the object of love or hope or thought; the secondary object was the mental phenomenon itself. Not all mental phenomena had primary objects, but all must have at least secondary objects. Thus, in the case of mood, the object of the mood was the mood itself. For if the mood were not, so to speak, aware of or directed towards itself, it would not be a conscious mood at all. Thus the definition of a mental event, as that which has an object, is saved. There could be no mental event which was not at least self-aware.

This somewhat implausible solution to the problem is not without importance for the later development of Existentialist psychology. Sartre maintained that along with all mental activity there must necessarily go a minimal self-awareness. And this led him, as it had led Brentano, to maintain that an unconscious mental event was a contradiction. This ruthless dismissal of the unconscious had other motives in Sartre's philosophy; but for Brentano it arose directly out of his definition of the mental as that which was directed to an object, whether primary or secondary.

Husserl was doubtless right to affirm the dependence of phenomenology on descriptive psychology, and it is to the descriptive element, somewhat loosely interpreted, that Existentialism also owes most. But in between the descriptive psychology of Brentano and the work of Heidegger, Merleau-Ponty, and Sartre stands Husserl himself. We must now try to see what uses he made of Brentano's definition of the psychical, or perhaps what changes he made in it, in order to produce phenomenology proper.

Brentano had maintained that the basic task of the philosopher was the description of psychological, as opposed to physical, facts; and that these facts were characterized by their intentionality or objective reference. Husserl, in the first place, did not accept the distinction between the psychological and the physical. Perhaps it would be less misleading to say that he ceased to be particularly interested in the distinction, and therefore it dropped out. Husserl thought that there was a parallelism between the structure of a subjective act and its referent which made both equally and together the proper study of the philosopher. For example, in the field of logic, he wished to study both the subject's immediate experience of deducing, and also at the same time the logical laws which enable a valid deduction to be made. He did not wish here to distinguish between the act and the object. *Cogito* and *cogitatum* are both manifestations which must be described. Moreover he was interested only in those mental acts which did in an obvious sense have an object; and, as he did not care particularly about distinguishing the mental from the physical, he was able to abandon intentionality as a criterion, or as a necessary and sufficient condition of the mental. He simply chose to consider those mental acts which *did* have objects, and to omit the rest. He was thus able to abandon the artificial complication of primary and secondary referents.

There are other features of his phenomenology which arise out of this same indifference to the question of whether objects exist as mental or as physical entities, or whether indeed they exist at all. Phenomenology was, he maintained, concerned with the description of 'pure' phenomena, with 'experiences', quite regardless of whether these experiences refer to concretely existing objects, or to fictions, or to themselves. This purity is ensured by the deliberate refusal of the philosopher to make any assertion of existence, whether physical or mental, about any of the phenomena under investigation, while he is investigating them. Husserl writes: 'From the beginning, and during all further steps, phenomenology does not contain in its scientific statements any assertion about real existence.' This is the beginning of the phenomenological 'reduction' (the *epoché*) to which we must return in a moment. It consists in putting on one side (in brackets) all that is known, or normally assumed, about the objects of perception or thought, in order to describe and, later, to analyse them as pure phenomena.

Finally, Husserl, as his theories developed, came to give a very much more complicated meaning to intentionality itself than just that of there being an object for a mental act or event. Gradually the doctrine emerges that by our intentional act we create as an object for ourselves what would otherwise have been mere chaotic, non-recurring, indescribable data. Intentionality no longer describes the simple relation between our glance and what we glance at; it takes on the more constructive, and much more Kantian, role of being that feature of our looking at the world which brings it about that there is a world of objects for us to look at.

At this point it is necessary to distinguish between different stages in Husserl's phenomenology. Everything which has been said so far refers primarily to the early phenomenology, as it emerged under the influence of Brentano, though, as we have seen, with simplifications and additions. It is necessary now to try very briefly to trace the historical development of Husserl's thought, in order to bring out those features of it which form the essential background to Existentialism. This task is by no means easy, and in the interests of brevity I must have recourse to very gross simplification of the issues.

Husserl started as a mathematician and logician, and in this field his main aim was to argue against psychologism, the interpretation of logical and mathematical truths as a kind of psychological truth. Here, right at the beginning of his career, there emerges an important difference between himself and Brentano. For, though Husserl sometimes used, of his own work, Brentano's expression 'descriptive psychology', in fact, from the beginning, he wished clearly to distinguish between the roles of psychology and philosophy. As we shall see, in attempting to isolate the intentional content of consciousness, he was never merely trying to produce accurate psychological descriptions of what was 'in the mind'. Indeed perhaps his greatest contribution to philosophy was his absolute insistence that such a description was impossible to conceive.

Husserl's first major publication was the *Logische Untersuchungen*, which came out in two volumes in 1900 and 1901. It was here that the first version of phenomenology appeared, with those divergencies from the interests of Brentano which have already been noticed. After this there came a period of over ten years in Husserl's life when, though he was constantly working at philosophy, preparing lectures and teaching, he actually published practically nothing. Then in 1913 the first volume of *Ideen* appeared (volume II and the sketch of volume III were published posthumously in 1950). We may use the term Transcendental Phenomenology for the developed doctrine of *Ideen*. Husserl used this term himself but did not exactly define it. Alternatively, he spoke of Pure Phenomenology, which perhaps, with its Kantian overtones, is the name which should be preferred. Finally, after 1913, there came a stage in Husserl's thought in which he was particularly concerned with the problems of intersubjectivity, and the effect of society upon a man's awareness of the world.

In the *Logische Untersuchungen*, then, we find the beginning of the 'reduction', the *epoché*, which is the first characteristically phenomenological method. Its aim is to eliminate presuppositions, and to turn experience into 'pure phenomena'; we also find that a new sense has been given to 'intentionality'. The first suggestion appears of the constructive or constitutive role of the intentional act, the act of perception. This new concept of the intentional act is explained by reference to its function, which is now described as the discovery of *meanings*.

In the first part of the *Logische Untersuchungen*, Husserl analyses the phenomenon of understanding a meaningful verbal expression. We hear or read, on a number of different occasions, a word, which we identify each time it occurs as the same word, that is as having the same meaning. Here then, is the first distinction which has to be drawn, namely the distinction between the *plurality* of a perceptual experiences and the *unity* of the meaning. But there is a further distinction between the *object which is meant* by a word, which is identical whoever uses the word, and the *object as it is meant*, which will vary between one speaker and another. 'Greenland' is a single object whether I, who am almost completely ignorant of Greenland, say the word or an explorer says it, who knows all that there is to know about Greenland. What is different in the two cases is not the object meant, but the object as it is meant. And Husserl further illustrates his distinction by the case of the two expressions 'the victor of Austerlitz' and 'the initiator of the French legal code', in which the object meant, Napoleon, is one, but the object as meant is not identical in the two expressions.

For the present purpose, the interest of this analysis lies in its generalized application. For Husserl moves from the consideration of our understanding of verbal expressions to our perceptual experiences of the world, and argues that, just as a multiplicity of meanings may be related to the same object meant by a word, so in an act of perception, one thing perceived may be related to many things *as they are perceived* (perceptual *noemata*). Of these *noemata* he refuses to ask whether they are real or unreal, physical or mental entities. No affirmation or denial of existence is made in referring to *noemata*. But just as a word relates to an object only because it is understood as meaning something, so a group of perceptual experiences relate to one definite perceived object only because they are 'animated by a certain way of comprehending and "intending"'. It is the function of intention to relate different perceptual experiences, or perceptual data, to one object, an object which is described as 'transcendent' to the act of perception. This object is identified in the intentional act of perception; that is to say, if one looks at an object from a variety of different angles over a period of time, it is the intentionality of perception which entitles one to say, 'I have been looking at the same object all this time.'

There is not perhaps any very exact analogy between the sense in which a word is understood to refer to an object, and the sense in which an experience or perception is understood to refer to an object. Indeed the longer one tries to work out the analogy with any exactitude, the more unsatisfactory it appears. However it is important to notice the use to which Husserl put the analogy. Just as one may, in many cases, grasp an object such as a triangle, only through a word with meaning, so we can grasp a perceptual object, such as a house, only through perceptual experiences, which are taken not as mere random phenomena, but as meaning something, as directed towards something. We cannot analyse the perceptual experience of seeing a house without employing the concept of meaning.

We are now in a position to see how the Transcendental or Pure Phenomenology of Husserl's later writings arises out of the earlier. The link is in this same concept of meaning. It is inevitable that discussion of meaning should lead at some stage to a discussion of universal or general essences. What is it that we mean when we refer to something (the same thing) either as a 'horse' or as a 'solid-hooved quadruped of the genus equus'? What is it that we mean when we describe a number of different things as all of them white? Husserl's concern with the problem of universals, though in a way it arose in the context of the discussion of meanings, was in fact relevant (as we have seen that the concept of meaning itself was) to his view of perception, to our awareness of things rather than words, and to our understanding of the world rather than of language. He argued that there is a special kind of experience, which is genuinely immediate experience, in which universals or general essences are grasped. He did not deny that one arrives at the notion of whiteness from the observation of many particular white objects. But he argued that in seeing a particular white object one is in fact seeing the essence; one is, that is to say, seeing *whiteness*.

It was this conviction that there is a kind of universal element in experience which led to his final abandonment of the descriptive psychology of Brentano. For Brentano had tried to confine himself to the description of the content of consciousness, to whatever is in the mind of a conscious person. His efforts had all been directed towards the isolation of what was 'immanent', or given, as an object of experience. Husserl now discovered that he could not identify the 'given' with the 'immanent'. There certainly were items given immediately in experience, which nevertheless pointed beyond the immediate experience and which were significant precisely because they referred to something beyond themselves. In a series of lectures written in 1907, and published in 1947 under the title *Die Idee der Phänomenologie*, he considers the case of my perception of a sustained musical note. If I turn my attention to the content of my consciousness at a given moment and try to describe it, what I am aware of is an experience of sound *now*. But it is equally certain that I perceive the sound as a part of a single sustained note; that is, though at any one second I cannot hear more than can be, as it were, contained in that second, yet I hear the note not just as sound, but as entailing a past and a future of similar sound. I am immediately aware both of the sound quality, *and* of the object, the note itself. But this object is not 'in' the mind. It is not 'immanent', but 'transcendent'. Moreover this transcendent object is general. It is a note, perhaps the F above middle C, which can recur and be re-identified as the same note.

From the point of view of Brentano's descriptive psychology, the general can never be immanent, in the mind, and Brentano never satisfactorily settled the problem of how he should speak of objects of thought when they were general or imaginary or in any way other than ordinary physical objects. Husserl on the other hand, while agreeing that the general was not in the mind, insisted that it could be immediately given in experience, indeed that the content of consciousness was itself perfectly unintelligible unless it was thought of as 'meaning' the general. The second-by-second awareness of the musical note is nothing, it is at most the awareness of mere sound, unless it is taken as meaning or pointing to the sustained note which is made up of these moments. Yet the hearer does not have to argue that the sounds make up a sustained note. He hears at once that they do so. Husserl asks: 'Could a divinity, an infinite intellect, have more knowledge of "red" than that he simply looks at it?'

The reduction, which was perhaps at first designed to remove from the mind all scientific knowledge, and anything whatever which would prejudice the question of the existence of the object of consciousness 'in' the mind, now has as its aim the removal of presuppositions, which might prevent the direct and immediate awareness of essences. The *Wesenschau* is a quite distinct experience, which now becomes the chief part of the philosophical method.

This *Wesenschau*, which is the grasping of essences, is also, by the time that *Ideen* came to be written, thought of as a productive or constitutive process. Just as objects of perception are constituted by experienced phenomena, which all signify or mean those objects, so acts of perception of objects go to make up awareness of general essences which are constituted by the consciousness as it grasps the meaning of the perception of particulars. There seems, in fact, to be a kind of hierarchy of meaningfulness. Individual experiences would be momentary and meaningless if they were not thought of as 'meaning' the object to which they are all to be referred. And objects themselves perceived individually would be unintelligible if they did not in turn reveal their meaning, that is the *eidos* or general essence which can be grasped in them. Husserl is not, I think, suggesting that essences exist in any sense alongside the ordinary world of concrete things, though he has sometimes been accused of the grossest forms of Platonism. He is rather saying that our awareness of the world, which is an intelligent and understanding awareness, could not be so unless we grasped the essences of things. This is what leads him to say that the grasping of essences is the prerequisite and necessary foundation of any empirical science whatever. No factual science could exist unless what was necessary for understanding the world of phenomena existed.

Naturally there are difficulties in the way of accepting any philosophical method which consists so largely in the grasping of essences or in intuition. How is one to distinguish the genuine from the fake intuition? How is one to know whether one has come upon a genuine essence? As usual in philosophy, future difficulties are concealed by taking the example of colour as the first example, by which to introduce the *Wesenschau*. It may seem plausible to speak of grasping the essence of red immediately, upon looking at one or more red objects, but, it may be argued, it is very different where the essence must be supposed to be more complex.

In a supplementary preface to the second edition of the

Logische Untersuchungen Husserl attempted to explain what his philosophical method amounted to (he had by then already formulated the method as one of intuition in *Ideen*, and had enunciated it as 'the principle of all principles'). He here warns his readers

not to hunt deductively for constructions irrelevant from the matter in hand, but to derive all knowledge from its ultimate sources, from principles seen authentically and understood as insights [*selbstgesehen und eingesehen*]; not to be diverted by any prejudices, by any verbal contradictions or indeed by anything in the whole world, even under the name of exact science, but to grant its right to whatever is clearly seen, which thus constitutes the 'origin', or what precedes all theories, or what sets the ultimate norm.[1]

There is an extraordinarily familiar and Cartesian ring about this injunction to reject all but clear and distinct ideas, and rest the whole of science upon them alone. But the problem of identifying one of these authentically understood principles, one of these given insights, is no nearer to being solved.

It is probable that Husserl would have thought that one could be sure to accept only genuine intuitions if and only if the reduction or *epoché* had been properly carried out. The area in which the reduction must primarily be carried out is the area of ordinary perception of the world; for what we have to 'put in brackets' is our ordinary beliefs about the existence of things in the world, the assumptions about existence which accompany both common sense and empirical science. When these assumptions have been put aside, we can concentrate on the concrete phenomenon before us, and only then will we be able to grasp its essence.

So far there is really nothing in the phenomenological reduction which was not contained in Descartes's Methodic Doubt, according to which, in the *First Meditation*, he proposed to call into question everything which he had ever been taught or which he had ever assumed to be true, in order to find some ideas so clear and distinct that he could not doubt them. But just as Descartes in advocating the method had a particular end in view, namely that enough would be resistant to doubt to entitle him to start to rebuild a 'marvellous new science' on strictly geometrical lines, so Husserl appears to have thought that the practice of the phenomenological reduction would lead in a particular direction. Perhaps the clearest statement of the goal is to be found in his *Cartesian Meditations*,

---

1 *Tijdschrift voor Philosophie*, i (1939), 116–17 (trans. M.W.).

Essence.

which were a version of some lectures which he delivered at the Sorbonne in 1929. In these lectures, Husserl argued that the upshot of 'putting the world in brackets', or performing the *epoché,* would be to show how the ordinary objective world was dependent upon the perceiving and thinking subject. The world whose existence has always been taken for granted by me, and which I have always experienced as an independent, objective phenomenon, will be shown to be given both existence and intelligibility or sense by my transcendental Ego—that is by the self which is left over when all my normal and common assumptions have been stripped away. The goal of the *epoché* may be said to be transcendental subjectivity. *Break Conditioning*

But we may still ask what is this subjectivity, which is left to be explored after the *epoché* has been completed, the uncovering of which Husserl claims as a total new beginning in philosophy? There are, it appears, three elements in what is left. There is the 'I' who thinks. This is not 'I' in the sense of a particular person, who has had a particular history, and who lives in a particular place. It is that 'I' of which I must be at least minimally aware in all my thoughts. It is the 'I' which is in Kant's phrase 'the vehicle of all concepts'. It is the 'I' which Descartes discovered when, in considering the piece of wax, he concluded that he must know himself who made judgements about the wax better than he knew the wax itself. The second element is the mental acts of this thinking subject; and lastly, not wholly distinguishable from the second element, there are the intentional objects of these mental acts, the *cogitata* of the *cogito.* These are the objects constituted by the activity of the transcendental Ego.

The true aim of the phenomenological *epoché* can perhaps be seen to be the unravelling of the constitution of objects. In attempting to rid ourselves of all preconceptions, and in particular of preconceptions about the reality or otherwise of objects in our world, we uncover the way in which these objects have been constructed by us (or have constructed themselves) as the sense or meaning of our immediate experiences. Rather as, in the thirties, new light seemed to be thrown on, for example, political thought by the dictum that the State was a logical construction out of the individuals who were all members of the State, Husserl may be thought to be inviting his readers to perform a far more severe dismembering of things normally taken as objects in our world, in order to show how they were constructed, out of what materials, and with what help from the constituting intellect. Since it is the transcendental Ego which is the source of the meanings which we ascribe to things, the transcendental reduction will allow these meanings to be examined. To raise the question whether Husserl is or is not an idealist, does or does not intend us to believe that objects exist in the world independently of any observer, seems to me to be unnecessary. Certainly we cannot depopulate the world of objects by merely wishing to do so. In that sense objects are independent of us. But if the question is raised, 'Would the world contain objects as it does now, if all the conscious people were swept away?' then the answer is that it would do so in exactly the same way as it would continue to contain words and sentences after all the people had gone. What would be absent would be significance.

In the last years of his life there were two problems which particularly concerned Husserl, both of them connected with the way in which consciousness constitutes its own world. The first was the problem of Time. We have seen already that Husserl's argument in favour of the direct perception of essences was based first and foremost on the inadequacy of Brentano's account of our perception of a long sustained musical note. That we perceive the sound, at any given moment, as implying its past and its future seemed to Husserl to show that we perceived it as a sound of a certain duration, and not just as a series of momentary bursts of sound. At the time when he used this example he did not lay any particular emphasis on the perception of duration itself as important in our constructing of objects, but doubtless his growing admiration for Kant led him to regard this as an increasingly urgent matter for study. And as far as the evidence so far available goes, it looks as if the greater part of the work which Husserl did in the thirties was on this subject. He came to believe that the transcendental Ego produced for itself the conception of time which carried with it the notion of duration and objectivity. Thus not only could the constitution of the whole world be derived from the activity of the transcendental Ego, but it could be derived from this one unique element in its activities. If one understood the genesis of the concept of time, one would understand everything.

The second problem was that of other people, how we know that they exist, and what the relation is between the transcendental Ego and other persons in the world. This can also be regarded as an aspect of what, as I have suggested already, was to become increasingly the preoccupation of Husserl and of phenomenology in general, namely the inquiry into the constitution of objects in our world. The evidence of Husserl's view is, once again, less than complete on this topic. But the problem of other people (or intersubjectivity) was discussed in the last of the *Cartesian Meditations* (Meditation 5) which was published posthumously in 1950. Husserl's treatment here of the world as a world essentially inhabited by other people was perhaps the part of his philosophy which had the profoundest effect on the development of Existentialism, particularly on the Existentialism of Sartre. Setting out the problem of my awareness of others he says:

Thus the problem is stated at first as a special one, namely that of the 'thereness for me' of others, and accordingly as the theme of a transcendental *theory of experiencing someone else* . . . But it soon becomes evident that the range of such a theory is much greater than at first it seems, that it contributes to the founding of a *transcendental theory of the objective world* and indeed to the founding of such a theory in every respect, notably as regards objective nature. The existence-sense of the world and of Nature in particular as Objective Nature, includes . . . thereness for everyone. This is always cointended wherever we speak of Objective actuality. In addition Objects with spiritual predicates belong to the experienced world. These objects, in respect of their origin and sense, refer us to subjects, usually other subjects, and their actively constituting intentionality. Thus it is in the case of all cultural objects (books, tools, works of any kind, and so forth) which moreover carry with them at the same time the experiential sense of thereness-for-everyone (that is everyone belonging to the corresponding cultural community, such as the European or perhaps more narrowly, the French cultural community, and so forth).[1]

There is a number of points in this passage which are of importance. First, by the *epoché,* by putting the world in brackets, Husserl seems to have suggested an inevitable solipsism. If I am allowed to claim knowledge of nothing but what is 'in' my consciousness, how can I allow for the existence of others? There should, it seems, just exist an undifferentiated world of sense-data experienced by me. But then two things become clear. First, a part of my experience is in fact an experience of other individuals like myself;

[1] *Cartesian Meditations*, v, trans. D. Cairns (The Hague, 1960), p. 92.

secondly, my experience of things in the world which I believe to be objective, to exist independently of myself and in time, can be shown to depend upon the existence of other people, who also observe them, and for whom they are also objects. Thus experience of the world absolutely entails the experience of more observers of the world than one, otherwise it would not be the world I in fact know. This is clearly true, Husserl argues, of the world of natural objects, but still more obviously true of objects which have a definite cultural role, or which are significant for human life in any number of different ways. Husserl speaks of our awareness of others as an awareness of monads, and the borrowing from Leibniz is justified by the specific point that monads *each* mirror the world. That is to say, we become aware, not only that human bodies exist as part of the world, but also that human *persons* exist, each having his own perceptions of his world, in which objects occur as they do in our own. Part of that which constitutes a thing which is an object for me, say a building in a street, is the fact that while I see the front of it, someone else sees the back; that while I think of it as the place I have to pass on my way back to work, someone else thinks of it as a centre of religious awe, or a place whose roof he once repaired. Neither the existence of the building as an object, nor its history, nor its function could be conceived if solipsism were true. But the building does exist as an object for the transcendental Ego, and therefore other people exist.

It is necessary to pause for a moment here to consider how revolutionary and how important for the future of philosophy this argument about other people actually is. Husserl's theory of our perception of the world is a complete break with the Cartesian theory, and by this I mean that it is a break not only with Descartes and his followers but also with the British empiricists. The only sense in which Husserl's *Cartesian Meditations* are Cartesian is that they claim to be scientific, and that they 'show the concrete possibility of the Cartesian idea of a philosophy as an all-embracing science grounded on an absolute foundation'. In all other respects they constitute, as does phenomenology itself, a total and general opposition to Descartes. For Descartes, the insistence upon a clear and distinct idea as the foundation of philosophy, though his appeal to his readers to cast aside all prejudice sounds superficially like the introduction of the phenomenological reduction, in fact led to two closely related difficulties. First, the ideas which seemed to fill the bill of clarity and distinctness best were mathematical ideas, and so he was set upon the path of trying to bring all knowledge into line with mathematical or deductive certainty. Secondly, and this is more important for our purposes, since he regarded ideas as the contents of the mind, and as having certain properties of their own (for instance clarity, obscurity, distinctness, confusability with other ideas, and so on) which were the only properties to be detected by a careful examination of them, the question arose how these ideas were related to anything in the world outside the mind. Notoriously, Descartes failed to solve this problem except by recourse to the goodness of the Deity, who would not give us ideas which so plainly *seemed* to be related to things in the outside world, if they were not really so related. The Cartesian problem thus can be seen to be that of relating what I am aware of to what there is; and of course this problem would not have arisen in this form if he had not insisted that the criterion of all knowledge was an internal criterion, namely that of the clarity and distinctness of our own mental content.

It is well known what form this self-same problem took in the thought of British empiricists. We should perhaps concentrate our attention on Hume (although Husserl himself was more impressed by the writings of Berkeley), since anti-Humean psychology characterizes all of French Existentialism, particularly that of Merleau-Ponty, as we shall see in due course. Hume's doctrine was that the whole of our conscious life could be seen to consist in two types of experience, the experience of having an impression and the experience of having an idea. Impressions are the basic raw materials out of which all thought and reasoning, as well as all perceptions, however abstract the thought or complex the perception, are made up. In reasoning we use ideas, which are fainter copies of impressions; in our perception of objects in the outside world we use impressions. But because an impression is fleeting, and simple, and of course dependent for existence on someone to be impressed, in order to construct for ourselves the objects in the world which we in fact perceive (objects, that is to say, which are durable, many-sided, and which exist whether we are there to perceive them or not), we make use of the faculty of imagination, which creates a feigned or fictitious continuity and solidity in objects—which indeed 'constitutes' them as objects, to use the phenomenologists' term.

It is easy to see how Hume, because of his commitment to the dogma that we experience nothing but impressions, was faced with a problem extremely like Husserl's own problem of explaining how it is that we experience objects as objects in the world, and not as mere parts of the contents of our own consciousness. If we reflect on the two elements in experience which Husserl came to think most essential to the solution of this problem, namely our awareness of time and our awareness of other people, we can see just how far he had moved from the unsatisfactory answer which Hume gave. (A complete study of Husserl's thought would at this point have to enter into a detailed analysis of his increasing preoccupation with Kant; but for our purposes there is the more limited aim of showing the extent to which, by whatever route, Hume had been left behind.)

Hume insists that by 'impression' he means a perception itself, a particular perception of scarlet or sweetness or pain. This is what we receive when, being awake, we open our eyes or in any way expose ourselves to the world. We are thus presented by Hume with a certain picture of man's relation to the universe which is not, in fact, a particularly plausible picture. For the suggestion is that our experience comes to us separated into units called impressions, which succeed one another like images on a screen. We simply receive them, in order. We may reflect upon the series of impressions, and thus make ideas for ourselves; or we may stop at the bare reception of the impressions, which are all of them in some sense of the same kind. That is to say, the stuff out of which our conscious experience of the world is composed is a uniform stuff, and completely different in kind from the ideas which we may afterwards form of it. It is true that some impressions are faint and so rather like ideas, while some ideas are strong and therefore like impressions. We may even confuse them one for the other at times. But nevertheless this is a confusion. It is like thinking in certain lights that a bat is a bird; it is a possible mistake to make, but indubitably a mistake. Impressions themselves, of their very nature, are without solidity, durability, publicity or intrinsic significance.

One may regard Brentano's programme of descriptive psychology as an attempt to discover in detail how unplausible such an account of our connection with the world is. His examination of intentionality, his attempt to show what is *in fact* the difference between hoping something, loving something, hearing something, and so on, all this is in direct opposition to the Humean view that our relation to the world is always the same, that we simply sit passively, as it were receiving the impressions as they come.

As a matter of fact there appears to be one place where Hume himself seems to be dissatisfied with the dogmatic dichotomy between impressions and ideas, and that is where he is writing about the moral sense. Our moral sense is, Hume says, a 'feeling or sentiment', and as such it is an impression, or rather a set of impressions, rather than a set of ideas. A stab of the moral sense is supposed to strike us immediately, like a stab of pain or a shock of pleasure or disgust. But Hume has then to face the question of how the moral sense of pleasure or the moral sense of pain is distinguished from any other sense of pain or pleasure. For obviously, if when we feel moral pleasure in the contemplation of some action, we immediately feel that the action is good, we have to be able to distinguish *this* kind of pleasure from the pleasure in let us say, wine or music, where equally we may say 'that is good', but not mean the same.

Hume has two parts to his answer to this question, both of which, it seems to me, tend to undermine his own dogmatic position. First he says that the specifically moral pleasure and pain arise only when we are aware of a particular kind of object, namely human characters and motives. This is supposed to make moral pleasure analogous to, let us say, pleasure in music, which is the peculiar kind of pleasure which arises only when we listen to agreeable music, and not when we look at a beautiful landscape. We are all perfectly accustomed, Hume says, to distinguishing one kind of pleasure from another by reference to their objects. Now this answer does suggest that there are some feelings which we have—pure impressions—which we cannot identify *except* by reference to an object; but the whole tenor of Hume's dogmatic philosophy was to show that we make the objects out of the impressions which we receive, which themselves should be in no way modified or distinguished one from another by a prior reference to an object. To distinguish the peculiar pleasure we derive from music from the peculiar pleasure we derive from an act of generosity might well be an exercise precisely in Brentano's descriptive psychology, for it seems that it cannot be carried out without the help of the concept of intentionality. Intentionality is, after all, nothing except the reference of our inner experience to an object.

Hume's second answer to the question fares little better. He says it is only when we consider an object in a particular way that it gives rise to the particular pleasure or pain which makes us call it *morally* good or evil. In order to give rise to a moral feeling, an object has to be considered in general, without reference to our own particular interests. (Hume, *Treatise*, Bk. III, sec. 2.) Here we seem to have something which is still further from a simple impression of pleasure or pain. For the suggestion is that we must first adopt a moral standpoint, that we must regard the character as something which has significance for human life in general, and *then* raise the question 'Is it pleasing or displeasing?', meaning thereby 'Does it please me if I imagine human life with such a character generally exhibited?'.

It is obvious that we are now being asked to regard the particular object, the generous act before us, as having a meaning, and as signifying generosity as a universal characteristic. It may be said that if we have an impression of green we are also, in order to identify it, obliged to regard it as signifying the universal greenness in general. But the case of generosity is different, because we cannot identify it as generosity—and therefore good—without going further along the path of abstraction; for we have to consider not merely that it *is* a characteristic which appears in many instances (this would be true of green as well), but that if it appeared more than it does, or if everyone possessed it, the world would be, not merely different, but better or worse. It is the realization that we are here dealing with a morally significant characteristic that I have referred to as 'adopting a moral standpoint'. And Hume seems to be reduced to saying that it is only when we have in this way grasped the *significance* of the particular that we can receive that impression, 'such a feeling or sentiment as denominates it morally good or evil'. His somewhat uneasy concessions that moral sense is a calm passion and therefore very like reason does nothing to mitigate the extreme awkwardness of this solution for the strict dogma of the distinctness of impressions from ideas.

Once that distinction is allowed to be broken down, then we may raise the question, as Husserl did, whether our consciousness of the world and our knowledge of it is not in fact riddled through and through with interpretation, whether objects are not in fact, all of them, constituted as objects for us in virtue of their significance for us. Our experience of the world, however strictly we perform the phenomenological reduction, may seem to be immediately and necessarily an experience of meanings.

Thus, to go back, other people appear in our consciousness, not merely as physical objects, not as hats and coats and umbrellas under which, we argue by analogy, there exist persons somewhat like ourselves. We do not hear human voices uttering words in the same way as we hear the clatter of engines or the lowing of cattle. Hearing a voice speaking is necessarily and immediately a part of an experience of an *alter ego*, a monad who himself reflects and interprets the world from his own point of view. We cannot distinguish an impression from an idea, for what we get immediately is a very complex perception of another person. Moreover, as Husserl argues, our whole conception of a world of durable objects which exist independently of ourselves and which are significant to us, used by us, and so on, is itself dependent on the recognition that these objects exist *for us and the others*, that they are available to other persons than ourselves. It is not that there is a sub-set of impressions in general which are normally grouped as impressions of other people. It is that other people enter our awareness of the world and constitute it, in an entirely new way. The Cartesian question was, how do we know, given that we have at best our own clear and distinct ideas and nothing else, that the world exists as we suppose it does; how are we to relate the content of our mind with the non-mental thing outside the mind? This Cartesian question has now been, not answered, but totally rejected. Through the concept of intentionality, it has become absurd to attempt to distinguish between the contents of the mind, as discrete examinable slices of experience, and the objects to which our consciousness is directed. In the course of the reduction in which the new philosophical method is to consist, we put on one side all our presuppositions about the world, and, as we have seen, all causal and scientific beliefs which we may need for ordinary life. But what we are left with is not a series of impressions. We are left with the transcendental Ego, which, at least in the later writings of Husserl, was above all the constituting agent of the world. We are left not with *our ideas* nor with *our impressions* but with *our world*.

We shall see later how this rejection of the Humean position developed, in French Existentialism, into a highly characteristic and subtle account of perception, both of the world at large and particularly of our own bodies, as the mediator between ourself and the rest of the physical world. For the moment there is need to mention one final feature of Husserl's later thought which, connected with his problem of intersubjectivity, leads to a characteristic interest of Existentialist philosophy. This is the idea of the *Lebenswelt,* or world of lived experience, which appeared with increasing frequency in the later posthumously published manuscripts. During his lifetime Husserl let fall only the vaguest hints of this concept. But Merleau-Ponty made an extensive study of all the articles which were intended to form the book. *The Crisis in European Sciences and Transcendental Phenomenology,* which was Husserl's last work, and which was not published in its entirety before his death. It was thus Merleau-Ponty who was largely responsible for introducing the idea of the *Lebenswelt* to Existentialism.

Briefly, the *Lebenswelt* is the world of lived experience, which will have its own peculiar style or structure, according to the social or cultural conditions of those who share it. It will be seen how the investigation of such a life-world may have arisen naturally, as a subject which followed from the work in the *Cartesian Meditations* on intersubjectivity. For there, as we saw, monads are related to each other primarily as reflecting the world of a particular time and a particular culture. Thereness-for-everyone, that which characterizes the objective world, is first of all thereness for everyone in France or everyone in Europe, everyone whose purposes can be assumed to be roughly intelligible to me. Husserl now thought that before the transcendental reduction and consequent analysis of experience could be undertaken by the phenomenologist, a kind of preliminary reduction was necessary, a suspension of science, so that the presuppositions of science could be exposed. The presuppositions are, if not socially determined, at least socially tied, in that the life-world just is the concept of the world as a whole as it is understood and interpreted by a particular social group.

This is one more stage in the long process of attempting to make sense of the notion of objectivity. In the *Cartesian Meditations* it was argued that there could be no world of objects without the existence of more people than one. Now it is argued that our conception of the objective world is dependent not only upon the existence of *some* other person, but on the existence of a group of which we are members. And it is supposed that we cannot analyse the objectivity of our world without finding out, not whether or not we share any presuppositions with the members of our group, but what these presuppositions are without which the world would not be our world. The *Lebenswelt* is the world categorized under the headings that we, at a particular time and place, as a matter of fact employ. Our aim must be, as philosophers, to discover what has later been called the 'logical framework' of our thought about the world, that is, to lay bare these categories. If we bear in mind this guiding thread in the later work of Husserl it will not perhaps surprise us to find that, in the end, Existentialism, which owed so much to him, has been virtually given up in favour of anthropology. Husserl himself was inclined to believe that he had been anticipated in the idea of the *Lebenswelt* by Lévy-Bruhl (see Merleau-Ponty, *Le Philosophie et la Sociologie*, 1951). However this may be, the line of connection between Husserl and Lévi-Strauss, through Merleau-Ponty, is clear enough. Existentialism rose and fell on the way.

— We Must be Members.

3
Martin Heidegger

BEFORE we pursue the development of Husserl's ideas in France, we must turn to examine another extremely important influence on Existentialism, that of Heidegger. Indeed it is wrong to speak of influence in this case, since there is good reason to treat Heidegger as the first true Existentialist, and therefore as the proper beginning of our study. However, he has himself rejected the title. In order to understand this, one need reflect only that philosophers' ideas very often change and develop during the course of their lives, and that, while it is perfectly legitimate to regard Heidegger as the author of one Existentialist text, his mature work could not be so described. There is the further fact to be noticed, which is that *Sein und Zeit*, the most 'existentialist' of his writings, is in fact incomplete. One may well suppose that it is precisely because he wished to organize his thought in a totally new way that he never finished this projected work. With these provisos, however, we may treat the early Heidegger as an Existentialist.

Heidegger's first philosophical work was his doctoral thesis on Duns Scotus, which was published in 1916; but after this, his next important publication was the first part of *Sein und Zeit*, in 1927. Immediately after this, he prepared a draft of an article on phenomenology for the *Encyclopaedia Britannica*, which was in fact never published, since he wrote it apparently on a suggestion from Husserl that they should collaborate over an article. But in the end Husserl's was the article published. There is an interesting difference between Husserl's article and Heidegger's unpublished draft. Heidegger introduces his exposition of the phenomenological method by a statement of the purposes of philosophy in general, which are, he says, to concern itself with 'being *qua* being'. He says of phenomenology that its importance lies in showing the need to reflect upon our *consciousness of being*; it realizes 'the necessity of a regress to consciousness', and it explores the field opened up during the regress. But essentially it serves ontology; it is merely a necessary preliminary to the proper philosophical task of exploring Being itself. 'We have to show that the manner of being of human existence is totally different from that of all other beings, and that it, in itself, contains in itself the possibility of the transcendental constitution.' To show this entails considering existence as a whole, and considering the existence of man in contact with the existence of other things. Phenomenology was not enough.

The supposition that there was anything left of philosophy after phenomenology is finished, that the subjectively based exploration of the transcendental Ego was not the whole of the subject matter of philosophy, was, of course, entirely contrary to Husserl's beliefs. And after the submission of this draft, there was no more collaboration between Husserl and Heidegger; indeed they met less and less frequently.

Heidegger's next published work was entitled *Kant and the Problem of Metaphysics* (1929), and this contained, as part of a detailed criticism of Kant, an attack on the limitations of the subjective method in philosophy. Heidegger described Kant as attempting to found metaphysics upon subjectivity—that is, upon an account of the appearance of the world to the observing and thinking subject; and he argued that this attempt is self-defeating. Kant's failure, he maintained, was the result of his limiting his notion of man to man's 'metaphysical nature'. He should have gone further, and considered the nature of man, not merely as an observer, nor even as a constitutor of his own world, but as a *member* of that world, as a complete being in time, with a history and a historical destiny. Husserl, writing marginal comments on Heidegger's Kant book, recorded his impression that by substituting this different, historical, concept of the human being for the pure transcendental Ego, Heidegger had turned philosophy, and in particular phenomenology, into anthropology. We may, if we like, once again see the whole rise and fall of Existentialism, including its final collapse into sociology or anthropology, foreshadowed in this comment.

There is one more short but important work of this time, namely Heidegger's inaugural lecture *What is Metaphysics?* (1929);[1] and here too, as we shall see in more detail in a moment, the fundamental problem of philosophy is said to be the *means of access to being*. Here the movement away from Husserl's preoccupation with the question of how the impersonal transcendental, consciousness constitutes the world for itself is yet more obvious. The nature of the being of man is central only as a means of elucidating a further problem about the nature of all being. It is no longer enough to consider how the world is constituted *for human consciousness*; one must consider how human beings, not merely human consciousness, can provide a clue to the nature of totally different kinds of being.

After 1929 there was a very long interval before Heidegger's next major work appeared, and this was a work of an entirely different kind, entitled *Holderlin und das Wesen der Dichtung* (1936). From this time on Heidegger has been more and more concerned with different ways of grasping Being, which have little or nothing to do with philosophical method as such. He has been increasingly given to the attempt to extract from language, and especially from the language of poetry, an insight into the Truth of Being; and, above all, he has attempted to present a picture of man as a questing problematic object in the world, with a history of his own, and exposed to the Truth of Being through 'thought-feelings'. He has rejected, therefore, the concept of the pure transcendental Ego, the undifferentiated 'vehicle of all concepts', and he has also rejected the idea that the world to be investigated by a philosopher must be the world seen from a certain point of view, from behind the eyes of an observer.

We have seen already how Husserl transformed the subjectivity of Descartes and of Hume, by refusing to accept the dichotomy between the content of the mind, and the world outside the mind; Heidegger would go further and attempt an account of the whole of the world as an historical phenomenon.

The further he moved from phenomenology, the less like an Existentialist he became. In an interesting essay published in 1949 entitled *Letter on Humanism*, he says: 'Since neither Husserl nor Sartre, as far as I can see thus far, recognise the essential place

---

[1] Trans. R. F. C. Hull and A. Crick, 1949. Published in *Existence and Being* (see p. 141 below).

of the historical factor in Being, neither Phenomenology nor Existentialism has entered the dimension in which alone a constructive debate with Marxism can take place.' It is worth noticing that Sartre who, in many people's eyes, appears to be the typical and complete Existentialist thinker, and with reason, has suffered rather the same fate as Heidegger. His Existentialism is contained almost entirely in one early book, *Being and Nothingness*, and later his writings have become more and more 'objective' until he has, to all intents and purposes, become a philosophical anthropologist; Marxism of a kind has in his case taken over from Existentialism.

If, then, we treat either Heidegger or Sartre as an Existentialist, we have to remember that we are referring to only a part of their total philosophical development. And, so far, we can see Heidegger's development as a progressive rejection of the phenomenological reduction, and of Husserl's theories of the constitution of the objective world. In rejecting this, as we have suggested, Heidegger necessarily rejected the attempt to isolate the 'transcendental Ego', the undifferentiated, pure 'I', who perceives and constructs the world, but is not involved in it. His concern, instead, was with Being, however we are to interpret this. Moreover it was precisely this concern which made him, in the end, reject Existentialism as well as phenomenology.

It seems inevitable, in considering the writings of Heidegger, that we should have to content ourselves with a less than precise interpretation. While Husserl's language is obscure and difficult, and his over-all project in philosophy quite as grandiose as Descartes's own, namely to found all knowledge on a scientific basis, the difficulties we encounter with Heidegger are different, and, to my mind, greater. For his writing is not intended to be precise, and his plan is not a scientific plan. In his later philosophy, he quite definitely aimed to demonstrate the power of poetical rather than logical thinking, and even in *Being and Time* his method is cumulative, and his actual vocabulary new and barbarous. Total comprehension would be impossible, and probably not what was intended. Like Hume's morality, Heidegger's philosophy is more properly felt than judged of. The task of exposition, then, is not easy.

I should perhaps briefly explain how I have attempted to do it. Most English books about Heidegger, or translations of his works into English, are rendered practically unreadable not only by the perhaps inevitable thick obscurity of the thought, but, particularly, by the number of new or newly-hyphenated words which appear. For example, when Heidegger wishes to refer to man's position in time, standing at the present moment, but aware both of past and future, he uses the work *Ekstasis*. But in order to bring out the element of 'standing back' involved in the meaning, he writes it '*Ek-stasis*'. Some commentators or translators simply do nothing with this, and write the word in German; others more unhappily still use the English word 'ecstasy', but in order to show that it does not mean what it normally means, they may write it as 'ec-stasy'. This seems to me monstrous. If Heidegger is saying anything which is intelligible at all, then it must be intelligible in English. Circumlocutions may, naturally, be necessary; but there cannot be any ground for inventing a new language. This must surely, in the end, be an obstacle to understanding. Moreover German is a language which can far more readily than English express complex concepts in single words. It is misleading and confusing to try to say what Heidegger says in German in the same number of English words. In the nature of the case we shall need more. I have not therefore attempted an exact English equivalent for all of Heidegger's technical terms; I have given the sense, in so far as I understand it, sometimes in one way, sometimes in another, but seldom in a one-word equivalent. There is only one concept about which I have tried hard to be consistent, and that is the central concept of the human being. Heidegger's word for human being is *Dasein*, literally 'Being there'. He wishes to emphasize, by the use of this expression, the fact that one cannot consider a human being except as a being in the midst of a world, an existent thing stuck there, so to speak, in the middle of other things. At a comparatively late stage in his development he takes to writing this '*Da-sein*' in order still further to emphasize the fact that this kind of entity has its place, *there*, in the world. I have made no distinction between '*Dasein*' and '*Da-sein*'; I have simply rendered both 'human being', since nothing else besides human beings are so designated by Heidegger. I have, moreover, taken the liberty of sometimes speaking of human beings in the plural; one of the more tedious aspects of Heidegger's own style is the necessity for everything to be referred to in abstract, and therefore singular, terms.

What is lost in this somewhat ruthless treatment of the text of Heidegger is first the atmosphere, created by the inventing of language as he goes along; and secondly the sense conveyed by him that by squeezing a literal meaning out of words long in common use, some new insight may be gained. But this seems to be an inevitable loss if one wishes to present the thought of Heidegger in a manner which bears any relation at all to the rest of philosophy.

To understand Being, would be to find an answer to the question why things exist at all, and in what manner they exist. Against every proposed solution, Heidegger could raise the objection that this had not gone far enough, that one needed to go behind this to a yet more fundamental explanation which would show how existence of a particular kind was possible. For he insists that one must not concentrate on particular existing objects, but upon Being-in-general—upon what, presumably, is common to all the different kinds of things in the world. It is easy to criticize this; sometimes the insistence on going further and further back, to raise over and over again the Kantian question, 'How is such and such possible?' looks like little more than a stylistic device, intended to produce in the reader a whirling impression of profundity, without particular sense. Notoriously, we cannot treat existence as a common predicate, like humanity or pinkness, which brings some things within a class and excludes others from it. The supposition that there is something common, which could be investigated, to the being of a leaf and the being of a triangle or a monkey seems absurd, and moreover to be the kind of absurdity which led Plato into difficulties a very long time ago. All this is true. But nevertheless if one is to understand the importance of Heidegger at all, one must remind oneself not to use too minute an instrument to probe him. It may be true that the problem he has posed is absurd, but his attempt to solve it is on so vast a scale that linguistic punctures here and there will have no effect upon it.

The nature of Being, then, was proposed by Heidegger as the proper subject matter of philosophy, and about this he never at any time changed his mind. The only thing that changed was his view of the proper way to pursue the subject. In *Being and Time* it is argued that we must approach it through the consideration of the nature of man, who stands in a peculiar relation to Being as a whole, because he and he alone of all beings can raise questions *about* Being. Since man is the only being who is capable of considering Being as a whole, he is in a unique way exposed to it. But man is the starting point only, and the original question is not epistemological, but ontological: it is concerned with what there is, not with how we know what there is.

Yet even the label 'ontology' is not entirely right. Heidegger wants to find out, not just what there is, but what is the *sense* of Being-in-general. There is obviously an ambiguity here. The question 'What is the sense of existence?' could mean 'What is the point or purpose of existence?' and it would be wrong, I think, to attribute exactly that question to Heidegger. It could also mean, less precisely, 'What is the significance of existence?', and this would be nearer the mark. It is because human existence (*Dasein*), besides being part of existence-as-a-whole, is also open to the experience that existence-as-a-whole has a *significance*, that the study of human existence comes first. In *What is Metaphysics?* Heidegger says: 'Man alone of all existing things experiences the wonder of all wonders: that there are things in being.' Herbert Spiegelberg, in attempting to throw light on the nature of Heidegger's inquiry, quotes an analogous passage from Coleridge, which seems to me to convey better than anything else what it is that Heidegger is after. The passage comes in *The Friend.* Coleridge writes:

Hast thou ever raised thy mind to the consideration of existence, in and by itself, as the mere act of existing? Hast thou ever said to thyself thoughtfully *It is!* heedless in that moment whether it were a man before thee or a flower or a grain of sand . . . without reference in short to this or that mode or form of existence? If thou hast attained to this thou wilt have felt the presence of a mystery which must have fixed thy spirit in awe and wonder.[1]

There are other passages in Coleridge which show that he was, from time to time, acutely aware of this 'wonder of all wonders'. This feeling, that there is something in the world to be explained, something which is amazing, is what, I suspect, leads many people in the first place to think that philosophy is what they would like to do, and what later leads them to become disappointed and disillusioned about philosophy; for the subject they want to study,

[1] *The Friend* (1809–10), in *S. T. Coleridge: The Complete Works* (Harper, New York, 1868), vol. ii, p. 463.

if it exists, is certainly neither epistemology, logic, nor morals. Perhaps Heidegger's fame rests largely on the fact that he too wants to study it, whatever it is.

The basic relationship between human beings and the world is that of Care or Concern (*Sorge*). If we can analyse what is meant by concern, we shall have gone a considerable way towards understanding Heidegger's early thought, and incidentally we shall have justified our treatment of him as an Existentialist, albeit one-time and partial. Concern is the significance which being in the world has for human beings, and it is moreover essentially connected with temporality, indeed the time structure of human life is the very same as the concern which human beings feel about the world. This is to say either that if a human being had no concept of time he would not be concerned or involved in the world in the specifically human way, or that the fact that human beings are aware of the passage of time by itself determines that their connection with the world is through concern. We shall return to the question of temporality in due course.

It is necessary now to raise the question of how concern was discovered to be the essential connection between man and the world, for only if we can clarify the method of its discovery can we say any more about what it actually is. In the second chapter of *Being and Time*, Heidegger introduces an account of philosophical method which he calls 'hermeneutic phenomenology'.

The term 'phenomenology' is here taken to mean the actual revealing of the truth about phenomena in the world, by examining them. He writes: 'The term "phenomenology" means primarily a concept of method . . . The title "phenomenology" expresses a maxim which can be formulated thus: "To the things themselves".' The phenomenon which has to be revealed is, of course, Being.

Most of us are forgetful of Being, in the sense that though, as humans, we are capable of experiencing the wonder and mystery of it, we are also immersed in it, and do not think of it as something which needs to be interpreted. We are surrounded by particular things in existence and forget to raise any question about existence itself. Phenomenological description interprets what we are immersed in, and opens our eyes to its significance. The phenomenological method is said to be 'hermeneutical' just because it does reveal significance. The world is thought of as a code or set of symbols, and the purpose of the phenomenological method is to interpret it. The particular part of the whole class of existent objects which is to be interpreted is, in the first place, *Dasein*— human existence itself. Thus Heidegger uses the expression 'hermeneutic phenomenology' as the name of a method which can be applied by human beings to themselves, and by means of which they can understand features of their perception and thought about the world which, without this method, they might have neglected, familiar to them though they are. It is by this method that concern is revealed in its crucial role.

The method thus sketched at the beginning of *Being and Time* is phenomenology only in a new, and perhaps loose, sense of the word; it is in fact Existentialist phenomenology, designed to reveal how things really are if we think about them, and to open our eyes to our true position in the world. The missionary, Socratic tone has come back, and the dispassionate scientific project of the phenomenological reduction seems far away.

Immediately one is bound to raise the question, 'What is the test of truth in a method of this kind?' Even if the phenomena to be examined present themselves, and no question of choice is involved, how can one be sure that the interpretation offered by hermeneutics is the right one? Perhaps the best one can do is to reply that an interpretation is true if it works, or if it is acceptable. There is an analogy between this method and the methods of psycho-analysis. It is plain, even at this stage, that there could be different interpretations of the phenomena of human life from Heidegger's, and that to a large extent a pontifical and grand manner must serve instead of argued justification in order to get his particular interpretation accepted.

Let us now consider what this first interpretation of the phenomena yields, and what is the nature of our concern with the world. Each human being is characterized by *Jemeinigkeit*, or individuality. This individuality is not a static quality of a person, but is a potentiality, a set of possibilities for every individual. Any human being is perpetually orientated towards his own possibilities. Among these possibilities are two kinds, under the heading of which all the rest can be organized: namely the possibilities of authentic and of inauthentic existence.

Heidegger says: 'The essence of human being lies in its existence.' Here we have the true voice of Existentialism. There is no preordained essential nature of *Dasein*; its essence lies in fulfilling its possibilities. But there are qualifications of this to be considered. It is not true that for any human being anything at all is possible; everyone is limited in their possible choices in some way or another. But we all of us have some possible choices, and our concern in the world is founded on the fact that we have to move forward from our condition at any given moment to another condition, in the future. Concern is our way of raising the question 'What shall I do?' or 'What can I use?' or 'Are things for me or against me?' —all questions which would not arise for a being who had no choice to make.

However, these choices are not made in a vacuum. They are made in the world; and the first two hundred pages or so of *Being and Time* are devoted to the phenomenology (in Heidegger's new sense) of *Weltlichkeit*: the worldliness, so to speak, of the world in which human beings exist. In the first place things are not presented to us just as material objects, but as tools for our purposes, or obstacles in our path. Then, more important, we do not find ourselves in the world alone, but surrounded by other people. Now we may fail to separate our own individual potentialities from the impersonal mass of mankind at large (Man, or people in general). We may accept, in our day-to-day life, all the standards, the beliefs and prejudices of the society in which we find ourselves. We may be content to wear ready-made clothes designed for people in general, to use public transport and public parks, to read newspapers written for people in general, and, in every detail of our lives, we may fail to distinguish ourselves from the mass. This is *inauthentic* existence. We do, necessarily, move forward in time and realize our possibilities—that is, we exist even in this form of life; but we convert our possibilities to inauthentic, impersonal, possibilities as we go along.

Authentic existence can begin only when we have realized and thoroughly understood what we are. Once we have grasped that human reality is characterized by the fact that each human being is, uniquely, himself and no one else, and that each of us has his own possibilities to fulfil, then our concern with the world, instead of being a mere concern to do as people in general do, to do things necessary for living as other members of our society live, can become *authentic* concern, to fulfil our real potentiality in the world. The concept of authenticity, of the necessity for each of us to realize his own uniqueness, is plainly very like the concept of in-wardness, or subjectivity, as expounded by Kierkegaard. It is precisely in this insistence upon the individuality of the life of each man, and the impossibility of his being satisfied with the second-hand, the *general* object, which would do for anyone, that the common character of Existentialism is to be found.

So far, Heidegger's conclusions have arisen from an examination of the phenomenon of man in society. But the interpretation, and with it the analysis of concern, proceeds with the description of certain key *attitudes* or *moods* with which we face our social situation. We can discover the meaning of our situation only by considering the way in which we are, as it were, attuned to the situation. We must analyse our *Stimmungen*, or moods, as a direct means of pursuing the end of discovering the nature of the relation between human beings and Beings-in-general, for part of the human exposure to the world is shown in the characteristic moods that he adopts.

It is important to notice here how widely Heidegger's analysis of moods differs from any that might be put forward by a psycholo-gist. It might well be that some moods (for instance grief or joy) might have been examined by psychologists and their nature and characteristics discussed. But in such an examination there would have been a sharp distinction between cognitive and emotional states, and moods would certainly not count as cognitive. Possibly because of the Cartesian commitment to basically epistemological questions, the nature of moods which were wholly disconnected from problems of perception seemed before Heidegger not to be a serious subject for psychologists and not to be a subject at all for philosophers. Heidegger's innovation was to regard a particular mood as the necessary way of recognizing a particular fact. The distinction between the cognitive and the emotional has broken down.

In recognizing that we are in a certain situation we thereby feel in a certain way. An important aspect of the phenomenology of this part of *Being and Time* is the distinction which Heidegger draws between two related but different attitudes, that is between fear and anxiety (*Angst*). We experience fear as we recognize some specific threat, constituted for us by our situation, typically a threat to our life itself. We experience anxiety, on the other hand, in the face of nothing in particular in our situation. We are driven by fear, and this is its sense or purpose, to save ourselves; we are driven by anxiety to drown ourselves in the trivial, the social, in all the ingredients of inauthentic existence. For there is an inauthentic counterpart to all the authentic ways of experiencing concern towards the world.

A man who is leading an inauthentic existence is in a condition of *Verfallensein*. He is in a fallen state. (But Heidegger is careful to say that he does not mean that the state is sinful.) Such a man ignores the reality of his own relation to the world. There is an ambiguity in his dealings with reality. He partly knows what things are, but partly does not, because he is so entirely caught up in the way other people see them, the labels attached to them by the world at large. He cannot straightforwardly form any opinion, and his statements are partly his own, partly those of people in general. If he seems to be interested in something, this is less because he is in pursuit of genuine understanding, than because of curiosity, a superficial and inconclusive motive. The conversation of the man who is inauthentic is said to be *Gerede* (prattle) as opposed to *Rede* (discourse).

It may be that a man can go through the whole of his life in the inauthentic state, and he may never emerge from it. But reflection may bring his attention to the true state of affairs and may open his eyes to his position in the world, which is above all a position of responsibility. Realizing, that is, the uniqueness of his position as a human being, he may see the force of his own reflective capacity, namely that he and he alone is responsible for the world's having significance. He may realize that while on the one hand his connection with the world is *necessarily* that of concern (for he would be less than human if he did not, for instance, have some ambitions, and regard some things as hindrances, some as aids to himself), on the other hand his concern could be of a different kind. In the unregenerate state, he accepts the significance which everyone else attaches to things. When he sees the truth about himself, he sees that people in general cannot really be the source of significance for *his* life. He is alone, and can attach what value he chooses to things.

It is at this point, at the threshold of authentic self-discovery, that the human being experiences anxiety. It is not anything in particular which afflicts him. It is simply his unsupported, isolated condition in the world. He begins to doubt the reality of the world, because he realizes that he is the source of its reality. Even his own place in the world is doubtful, and he cannot take anything for granted any more. In this condition of anxiety, he may, as we have seen, seek to protect himself by becoming yet more deeply engaged in the ordinary, the everyday and the practical. Fearing to leave his supports, he may throw himself entirely on the mercy of people in general, defend the orthodox, the bourgeois and the normal, and go on frantically pursuing his inauthentic goals. He may, on the other hand, determinedly change the character of his concern for the world, and, keeping before his eyes his lonely and responsible position, he may exercise resolution, and launch himself forward into authentic existence.

In order to make it a little clearer (though by no means wholly clear) what authentic existence is, there are two concepts, both related to the basic concept of concern, which must be further elucidated. The first is the concept of Nothing, the second that of Time. Both these concepts are elaborated first in *Being and Time* and then again in *What is Metaphysics?* and in *Kant and the Problem of Metaphysics*. Both are crucial to Heidegger's thought, and it is, moreover, hard to separate what he said about one from what he said about the other.

Let us start with Nothing. There is naturally a very great embarrassment which must be felt by anyone accustomed to trying to talk sense, or to think clearly, in even proposing Nothing as a subject for discussion. There is a deep Alice in Wonderland dottiness about it which is not encouraging. Perhaps 'Nothingness', being a term not in current use, might be a better translation of *Nichts*; or 'Non-existence' might be suggested, but neither is very good. For some of Heidegger's statements seem to require the ordinary word, and to rely upon the ambiguities, not to say confusions, which this generates. For part of what he means seems to be that, in order for a human being to consider the world at all (and it will be remembered that the peculiar role of the human being, as a clue to the nature of Being-in-general, consisted in his being able to consider the world), it is necessary for him to be able to think of separate beings, all of them different from one another and from himself. The notion that he is different from the things around him is connected with the notion that, however one describes the world, there will have to be an element of negation in the description. To find out the truth about things is to attempt to reveal them, and this is to show that they are *not* as they first appear. Moreover, as we shall see in more detail in a moment, the human being, in seeing himself in the context of the world, and different from other things in it, comes to realize that he is always moving towards some unrealized possibility. By merely staying alive, he is recognizing a future which consists of things which are *not yet real*. The very idea of change involves negation. What is going to happen is what has not yet happened.

All this is not clear in Heidegger (and we shall find this aspect of the concept of Nothing much more fruitfully discussed by the French Existentialists, particularly by Sartre). Indeed he is inclined to deny that the idea of Nothing is derived from the logical idea of negation. But it seems that what he is saying must be interpreted partly to mean that human beings discover, in discovering the world, that they think of Not-Being as much as they think of Being, and that the discovery and contemplation of Being-in-general has bound up with it the notion of what does not exist.

In one particular way, Heidegger insists that this is so. For the philosophical human being recognizes at a very early stage that he is mortal. This, obviously, entails the recognition of the truth that, sooner or later, he will not exist. Heidegger regards this genuine acceptance of the future non-existence of himself as the first step towards the authentic way of life. In accepting it, the human being recognizes that he is alone, distinct from every other person and object in the world, no longer able to turn for support to people in general. He must die his own death, by himself. So not existing at all is the final end towards which he is moving. In this sense *Nichts* means 'non-existence', or 'nothingness'.

The contemplation of his own future non-existence leads to the exploitation of the other, related sense of Nothing which seems to be necessary to Heidegger's picture of the world. He says: 'In anguish, the human being discovers himself confronted by the Nothing, which is the possible impossibility of his existence.' He suddenly realizes that he is, in a sense familiar from religious writers, *himself* nothing. He arises out of a chance which hurls him into the world, and ends in death when he will not exist any more. But besides his own nothingness, in this sense, the human being who experiences anxiety will be confronted by a kind of receding of ordinary objects in the world, so that they too will seem to cease to exist. Heidegger coins a verb, *'nichten'*, 'to

+ psychedelic experience = nothing.

nothing', for the event of the discovery by a human being of his insecurity in the world of ordinary objects, in which this anxiety comes into being, and which marks the end of his inauthentic existence.

Authenticity consists in a realization of one's position in the world, one's isolation, and one's inevitable orientation towards one's own death. Before this realization can be complete, one has to experience oneself as something suspended over a void. Things in the world must lose their solidity (and thus their attraction and apparent importance), and one must feel deep alarm at the vacancy which surrounds one. This, then, is the second and more dramatic sense of the word 'Nothing' which Heidegger uses.

Metaphors of the abyss, the void, and of vertigo spring to mind in order to elucidate this concept. It is, of course, very difficult to be sure that one has grasped the sense of it. As always, in reading Heidegger, one may fancy that one understands, but turning back to the text, one may quickly lose all confidence, since his language here, as elsewhere, is so full of neologisms, barbarisms, and plain confusion. However, in *Kant and the Problem of Metaphysics*, where the problem of Nothing is carried further than in *Being and Time*, he criticizes Kant on two counts, which may both amount to the same. First, as we have seen, he criticizes him because, like Husserl after him, he concentrated too much on the pure perceptive 'I', without taking into account his position as a human being in the world of things; secondly he is said to have gone wrong because he did not recognize Nothing as the only possible ground of analysis of Human Being.

Nothing is here connected explicitly with the finitude of human beings, their essential movement towards their own end in death. Kant is supposed to have thought that, though in one sense it was impossible to discover metaphysical truths (about the beginning of the world, or about immortality), yet in another sense it was possible to discover the forms and categories with which the human being approached the world, and with the help of which he perceived it and objectified it, necessarily. This, according to Heidegger, was too static a picture of man's connection with the world. Because of the necessary movement of the human being towards the end of his life, though he may think about ordinary things in the world in the manner for which Kant argued, there is nevertheless a quite different kind of thinking about Being-in-general, the possibility of which Kant entirely overlooked. Kant, Heidegger said, was the 'prophet of man's metaphysical finitude' simply because he raised the question of the possibility of metaphysics. But he did not take account of man's separation by the gap of Nothing from the things he perceived, or constructed as objects: human beings both have to be aware of the distance between ordinary things and themselves (and this, roughly, was the first sense of 'Nothing' that we noticed), and they have to be aware that things in particular, as opposed to Being-in-general, tend, as it were, to float away from them and disappear from view. The dizziness or vertigo induced by seeing things as they are, and seeing Human Being as it is, can be cured only by raising a further question, which Kant did not raise at all, about Being itself, in general terms.

Reaching the stage of raising such a question is what Heidegger refers to as 'going beyond metaphysics'. Thus 'Nothing' in the second sense is supposed to be essential for one who is to exercise his right, as a human being, to investigate Being-in-general. He must, both epistemologically and emotionally, recognize that he exists in a medium consisting of nothing. Heidegger says:

It would be immature to adopt the facile explanation that Nothing is merely the nugatory, equating it with the non-existent. We ought rather to equip ourselves and prepare for one thing only: to experience in Nothing the immensity of that which gives every being its licence to be. That is, Being itself.

It is because we can grasp, in a way, the unfathomable abyss of there not being anything, that we can consider the question why there are any particular things in existence at all, and hence raise the question of Being, or existence, in general. 'Nothing', in this sense, is perhaps properly analysed as 'the possibility of the non-existence of everything'. It is this, according to Heidegger, which Kant overlooked, and the grasping of which is a peculiar property of human beings.

Since the realization of man's finitude was the beginning of his recognition of the concept of Nothing, and since finitude meant the fact that he was mortal, it will be a little clearer now how the ideas of Nothing and of Time are linked. Over and over again, throughout all his writings, Heidegger insists that man is, above all, essentially a temporal being. It is perhaps in his discussion of time, more than anywhere else, that he induces in his readers that feeling of exasperation which has already been noticed as a characteristic, and indeed an inevitable, reaction to Existentialist philosophy. One feels inclined to say that he makes too much of the fact that people have a continuous existence, that is, that they have a past and a future; and too much of the fact that they are mortal, and their future does not extend for ever. He speaks of transcending the past towards a future, but what does this mean, one may ask, except continuing to exist for a period of time? He speaks of launching oneself towards death. But how can one help doing this, as long as one is actually alive, and not yet dead?

However, two things should be noticed. First, though this reaction is characteristic, also—characteristically—Existentialism achieves something precisely by getting us to concentrate upon some feature of our life which is already obvious, but frequently forgotten or taken for granted. Secondly, the subject of Time has always been both attractive to philosophers and trivial to non-philosophers, or to philosophers in the guise of plain men. Heidegger knows, and admits, that his concept of Time is remote from the everyday concept; but there may still be point in his expounding it. The common-sense view of Time should not be brought into direct conflict with Heidegger's theory in order to make it look absurd. One must first see how his theory arose, and how, if at all, it seeks to explain observed phenomena. (In the same way, G. E. Moore was wrong to try to demolish J. E. McTaggart's theory that Time was unreal, merely by saying that some events happened before others in the day. McTaggart knew this as well as anyone else, but was making a *further* point). Let us look, then, at Heidegger's theory of Time.

Temporality is the name of the way in which Time exists in human existence. There could be no concern (which, as we have seen, is the basic relation between human beings and the world) if there were no temporality. We are aware of the past, the present, and the future, in three different ways; and, in accordance with these ways, we are aware first of the 'facticity' of ourselves in the world (that is, such facts as where we were born, who our parents were, where we were educated); secondly, of the immediate business of the moment, what is actually before our eyes; and finally we are aware of our possibilities, towards the fulfilment of which we actually do things in the world. It is this last mode of concern, based upon our awareness of the future, which is the most important.

Concern with the world consists in the thought 'there is something to be done'; and such a thought entails the thought of a future time. If a human being is essentially always stretching out towards the next thing, then merely stretching out makes sense only if it is, as it were, informed with the general thought 'I will have this'. So interpretation of the world demands an awareness of future Time. Concern with the world and freedom to do things in the world are one and the same. A tree or a stone cannot be concerned with the world, precisely because they cannot see and aim to fulfil any potentiality in themselves. They cannot be, as a human being is, *creative* of their own essence.

Heidegger contrasts his view of the future with the ordinary man's view by saying that for common sense Time consists of a series of instants, each now, or about to be now, and each valued separately. He argues that the future is not a mere set of instants each of which is about to become the present instant, but rather that the existence of future time actually determines, and is logically prior to, present time. (And indeed it seems to me that at least this much might be argued, that one could not conceive of anyone with a grasp of what was meant by 'the present' who did not also, in a more primitive way, grasp what was meant by 'past' and 'future'). The plain man, the man in the 'fallen' or inauthentic state, if he thinks of time at all, thinks of it as primarily present. He is absorbed in what is actually in front of him, and he regards the past as relatively uninteresting, and the future merely as what will soon be present. But the present, for the authentic human being, is a synthesis of past and future, since he knows what he was, and what he resolves to be, and it is this upon which he is concentrated. This self-knowledge is referred to by Heidegger as *Gewissheit*, which is often translated 'conscience'. We are said to be drawn by conscience towards our final solitary goal, which is death. But this does not mean that there is anything which conscience dictates to us as having to be done. This is why, in a way, 'conscience' is a misleading expression, though it may well have been specifically chosen by Heidegger for its moralistic suggestions. He is suggesting that if a human being is aware of himself as a being based on the facts of his past and also as projected towards the future which he chooses, then he will take full responsibility

In talking about consciousness, we are talking about death.

for his life, and he will recognize that his choices are his own, not dictated any longer by what people in general do or expect. Conscience will thus display to him the significance of his acts, as part of his own unique and chosen path through life. This awareness of significance can be achieved only if a man has first passed through the phase of anxiety, where he is oppressed by the insecurity of himself in the world. So true self-awareness brings together the concepts of Nothing and of Time, which together determine the nature of the human being's relation to the world, his concern with it.

So far our attempted exposition of the hermeneutic phenomenology of *Being and Time* has been entirely concerned with Heidegger's analysis of human beings. But even in the unfinished *Being and Time* he says things which point to the question for the sake of which this analysis of Human Being was undertaken, namely the nature of Being-in-general. Human beings were characterized as uniquely capable of raising the question what is Being-in-general, and thus their nature was to provide a *clue* to the nature of Being-in-general. Everything which has so far been said about temporality, for instance, makes sense only with reference to specifically human existence, as do all the related descriptions of concern. But it seems that Heidegger wished to assert some kind of parallelism between the temporality of the human being and the time structure of Being-in-general. In so far as this is intelligible, it seems to suggest a dynamism in everything that exists, such that it would never be possible to describe a moment of Being as if it were a state of isolated things. This seems to be at the root of his criticism of Kant, who, according to Heidegger, supposed that he could lay bare once and for all the categories and the structures by which things were objectified for people, whereas on the contrary human beings, in grasping the possibility of non-existence of things, also grasped that things were finite, and that they changed in time. But it is necessary to admit that this is very obscure. What does Heidegger mean when he says that things themselves change and develop in time? Does his criticism of Kant amount to saying that one could never fix on categories according to which one must think, for ever, since the categories of thought will change with the course of history?

If this is what he saying, then it is intelligible, but it gives force to Husserl's suspicion that for Heidegger, philosophy was gradually giving place to anthropology. For it looks as though the very most that anyone could do would be to lay bare the structure of thought about objects at a particular time in the history of mankind. This is borne out by the fact that Heidegger denies the desirability of Husserl's goal, a presuppositionless philosophy. He said that one should retain one's presuppositions and simply demonstrate what followed from them. A timeless, once-for-all analysis of what lies behind our thought about the world is a chimera. 'Philosophy will never want to contest its presuppositions, but also will not allow itself merely to admit them. It understands the presuppositions and brings that for which they are presuppositions into unity with them, to an impressive unfolding.' The hermeneutic method consists precisely in revealing the true meaning of what are, and must inevitably remain, presuppositions.

At the end of *Being and Time* Heidegger introduces another concept, closely related to that of temporality, namely the concept of history. Heidegger has himself later suggested that this last published chapter is the most important of all, and shows the way in which, from the study of human beings, we may move on to the study of Being-in-general. It is not entirely easy to see any difference between the idea of the historical nature of human beings and their temporal nature. As we have seen, Heidegger believes that, starting by being, as it were, thrown into the world, a human being necessarily progresses, by himself, towards the final event which is his death. If he has authentic existence he is aware of himself as poised between his past and his future, but he is determined even more by his future than by his past. So much is true for every individual man. But it is also true that Being-in-general has a history, and one which, like an individual man's history, is not a mere passively awaited set of occurrences, but is something fixed and created by Being itself. That is, the use made of the past will determine the future of Being-in-general. But to say this is certainly to commit oneself to the view that without the concern of human beings there would be no history, and therefore no Being-in-general. For the notion that any but a human being could, in the phrase just employed, 'make use of' the past is absurd.

What is real and what has a history is whatever is revealed by human beings. As a human being understands more of the past, so he thereby incorporates it into his present plans and projects. So the history of things is discovered as a path towards the future.

It is not that one can learn from history, or that history repeats itself. It is rather that by fully understanding what has happened once, one carries this understanding into one's resolutions for the future. Resolution is the awareness of one's destiny which can come only if one keeps both past and present in view. It seems that this is what Heidegger means when he says:

Because existence is thrown into the world as a matter of fact, the nature of history, as the quiet power of the possible, becomes more revealingly exposed, the more concretely and particularly past being is understood in terms of future possibility.

And again he says:

The theme of history is concerned neither with that which happens only once, nor with some generality which hovers over the facts, but with factually existent past possibility. Such possibility can never be related i.e. historically understood authentically as long as it is turned into the paleness of a model above time. Only factually authentic history, as resolute destiny, can so reveal past history that in the repetition the force of the possible will strikingly affect the way things are, that is will be allowed to affect the future.[1]

Resolvedness and understanding can allow us to recapture and literally re-acquire the past in the form of a tradition. Resolution itself is said by Heidegger to be a form of faithfulness, which leads to a kind of reverence for repeatable possibilities. *What* is revered will depend upon the free choice of the human being. Heidegger refers to the importance of the human being 'choosing his heroes'. But he does not, at least in *Being and Time*, offer any clue to the way in which these heroes are to be chosen, nor the difference it would make to the future whether this hero were chosen or that.

At least it is fairly clear how, looking back in 1949 over the development of his own philosophy, he can see it as equipped to some extent to come into head-on conflict with Marx's thought. He is at least playing the same game, and indeed perhaps playing it in the same language, as Marx. For his philosophy is concerned with the inevitable role of man among a surrounding field of *things in the world*. The resolution which is the essence of authentic existence is an assertion of human independence, both of things

[1] *Being and Time*, trans. J. Macquarrie and E. Robinson (London, 1967), p. 392.

and of other people in general. The domination by things in the world which marks inauthentic existence, as well as the confusion engendered by anxiety, is obviously analogous to the phenomenon of *alienation*, from which the dialectic of Marx was to set people free. The point at which Marxism seems a true conclusion of Existentialism is the point at which Existentialism allows history to enter into philosophical thought.

From the abandonment of *Being and Time* onwards, Heidegger's work became less and less systematic, and more poetic in its form. Being in general, to the investigation of which Heidegger was originally committed, now increasingly seems to be thought of as something to which people may be exposed, which may reveal itself to them in flashes of intuition. Sometimes Being is spoken of as itself something creative, in virtue of which all the particular things that exist do exist. There is a Platonic tendency to shift backwards and forwards between this view and the view that Being is that which is common to or shared by all existing things. But someone who is concerned only with particular existing objects is employing only 'calculative' and not 'creative' thinking, and this, Heidegger insists (as early as *What is Metaphysics?*), must always misrepresent.

In the end philosophy itself is replaced by what Heidegger calls 'thinking of Being'. This consists simply in recognizing that, as humans, we live in 'a clearing of Being', that Being can speak to us, if we have ears to hear. The poet-thinker is the shepherd or guardian of Being, and his pronouncements are presumably like the utterances of the oracle, the voice of the most holy, speaking through the medium of the elect. Into this area perhaps we need not follow Heidegger, since it is certain that Existentialism does not lie in this direction.

What, then, to sum up, is Heidegger's specific form of Existentialism? We can see, at least in his early philosophical writings, many of those elements which, in the first chapter, were noticed as essential to Existentialist thought. At the same time, though he departed very far from Husserl's phenomenology, he himself wrote that his philosophy could not have come into existence without Husserl. So we are entitled to regard Heidegger as the first philosophical Existentialist, that is, as the first to direct phenomenology into an Existentialist channel.

The most important development in this direction is the

introduction into phenomenology of the concept of freedom. This in fact is the change which seems in the end to have separated Heidegger from Husserl, and to have divided them by an unbridgeable gulf. Husserl was primarily concerned with the analysis of a subject's relation to his perceptual and emotional world at a given time. Naturally he had to raise the question of the subject's awareness of time, but this interested him primarily as part of the general question, 'How is the world made objective for the "I" observing?' If he could have solved the problem of the concept of time, as it appeared after the transcendental reduction, he believed he would have thereby solved the problem of the construction of objects in the world. But the starting point of this enquiry, necessarily, according to the rules of the reduction, was a *given present moment*. For Heidegger, as we have seen, the subject's relation to the future was more crucial that his relation to the present. The emphasis was no longer on a man's construction of the world here and now, but on his projection of himself towards the time to come.

Heidegger is more concerned with the category of the possible than of the actual. He is aiming to show, not how we come to be aware of what is now in existence, but how we bring into being something which *does not yet exist*. This is the true significance of his insistence upon the new category of the non-existent.

Now, obviously, the human subject does not merely think about the future which does not yet exist; his projection forward is *practical*. He actually brings about what is not yet the case. Thus it would not be misleading to view the development from Husserl to Heidegger as a development from the idea of cognition to that of action. And it is in this way that the human subject, in Heidegger, appears above all as a free subject, capable of *doing* things and *initiating changes* in the world.

The introduction of the category of the possible opens up a very wide philosophical field. In the first place, it opens the way for an ethical theory, because the human subject is now primarily thought of as an agent; secondly, perhaps more dubiously, it seems to open the way for a theory of aesthetics. For to be able to contemplate an object from an aesthetic standpoint seems to require a certain detachment from the world. Someone who was completely concentrated upon how things are at a given moment could not create a work of art, nor realize that what he was looking at or reading or hearing *was* in fact a work of art. The Existentialist insistence on what-is-not-actual leads naturally towards a theory not only of action in a possible future, but of representation of a possible, timeless, aspect of the world, that is, a theory of aesthetics.

But there is more to Heidegger's form of Existentialism than simply that it introduced the possibility of ethics and aesthetics, and added this to phenomenology. The particular kind of ethics is determined for him, and for Existentialism in general, by its being supposedly derived from a description of man's place in the world. This is why, as we have seen, *Being and Time* is the only specifically Existentialist work among Heidegger's philosophical writings, because it is aimed at exploring man's place in the world.

Next we should notice Heidegger's anti-Cartesianism. In the first chapter it was suggested that a kind of subjectivism is a characteristic sign of an Existentialist philosopher. This was there taken to mean that a man's personal feelings were to be taken as evidence of how things are, and as much weight attached to such evidence as to the evidence of shared knowledge. We can perhaps see a little more clearly now that the label 'subjectivism' is somewhat misleading. It is certainly true that Heidegger explores man's relation to the world as much through his moods as through his strictly cognitive powers, or through his perception. Indeed he moves towards the position where it is no longer possible to draw a distinction between cognition, emotion and will. This is anti-Cartesianism.

The Cartesian distinction between the inner (in the mind) and the outer (in the world) had already been destroyed by Husserl. Now Existentialism is to be seen further breaking down the very distinction between the mind and the body, between man as *res cogitans* and man as *res extensa*. There could be no more fundamental change for philosophy. A human being's relation to the world is a total relation of one thing among other things. Despite Heidegger's insistence upon the mood as a connection between man and the world, he is also attempting an analysis of this connection from a height so Olympian that the human being is just a part of Being in general. The characteristic of a human being is certainly that he must progress alone towards his unique destiny, his death. To this extent each man must be related to the world by his own connections with it and by no one else's. The realization of this truism is the secret of authenticity. But this is all that, in Heidegger, the personal and the subjective amounts to. What he is concerned with is the total engagement of each individual in the world, by thought, perception, feeling and action alike.

Finally, there is obviously in Heidegger's writings the Existentialist desire to shock his readers out of their complacent and unthinking ways, out of their unawareness of Being. The missionary zeal of the true Existentialist is nowhere more manifest than in him. The extent to which he is successful in getting people to reassess their position in the world is presumably dependent upon the degree to which they insist on understanding what is said to them before acting on it. Many may feel some sympathy with Herbert Spiegelberg who concludes his chapter on Heidegger with these words:

> Heidegger's obvious intent to awaken and even to shock his reader into a realization of the phenomena has all too often defeated his own purpose. The squeezing and bending of existing words by literalizing their meanings, whether etymologically justified or not, without additional guidance to the reader by way of definitions or examples, is apt to create a twilight of uncritical semi-understanding among the gullible, and of hostile misunderstanding among the more critical.[1]

It seems that, however many sympathetic attempts are made to relate Heidegger's philosophy to something more readily recognizable under that name, there will still remain a fairly hard core of sheer verbiage, which is not absolutely essential to Existentialist thought, but which has all too often seemed to form an integral part of it.

[1] *The Phenomenological Movement*, vol. i. p. 351.

4
Maurice Merleau-Ponty

FOR various reasons, social, political and literary, Existentialism is largely identified by English-speaking people with French Existentialism. It has been emphasized in the foregoing chapters that Existentialism has always been a practical philosophy, a morality in the sense that its acceptance was meant to affect conduct; and the image of the post-war Existentialist student, though loosely connected with philosophy, is nevertheless not without connections. The characteristic Existentialist mood was properly expressed in actual French students, as well as in the novels and plays of Jean-Paul Sartre. It is right to think of this mood as peculiarly French, however clearly its origins were German. The rest of this book will therefore be devoted to a fairly detailed discussion of French Existentialist philosophers, and particularly to the philosophy of Sartre himself, in whom, one could argue, Existentialist thought reached its limit and also met its death.

First, however, it will be desirable to examine rather more briefly the work of his colleague, co-editor and friend, Maurice Merleau-Ponty, who, though without the immense power of imagination which distinguishes Sartre, was in some ways a more serious philosopher than he, and may indeed be considered the philosophers' Existentialist. It is somewhat paradoxical to consider Merleau-Ponty before Sartre, for it was Sartre, and not he, who first introduced Husserl to French philosophers. Moreover Sartre was older than Merleau-Ponty by a few years, and, not only was Sartre's great Existentialist work *Being and Nothingness* published before Merleau-Ponty's *Phenomenology of Perception*, but the last part of the latter work was a specific criticism of the former. For all these reasons, Sartre should come first. On the other hand, though Merleau-Ponty, who died in 1961, had embarked on a book, *The Visible and the Invisible,* which seems to have pointed towards a very grandiose aim of discussing and interpreting Being in general, after the manner of Heidegger, there is not enough of this project completed for it to be judged. We must therefore think of him as the author of the *Phenomenology of Perception,* and this is a good introduction to the Existentialism of France.

All the same, there are some respects in which he is not typical. He is serious but not prophetic; he is deeply interested in his subject, but in no sense missionary; and though his work has some bearing on ethics, it shows none of the influence of either Kierkegaard or Nietzsche. Nevertheless, we may see in his work the tendency to draw from a variety of sources and to tackle a variety of subjects which is both characteristically Existentialist and characteristically French. Though he did not, like Sartre, write philosophical novels or plays, nor, like Gabriel Marcel, write philosophy in the form of a journal, yet, compared with English-speaking philosophers, he was still unacademic. Indeed this lack of academic rigour constitutes an obstacle to understanding. The undertakings may seem to us too vague, the standards of proof too low, the actual time and trouble taken on ensuring correctness or economy of argument too little. His writing is certainly excessively repetitive. It is, however, consistent, and it is possible to discern a clear line of argument, starting in his earliest book. This argument may, without too much parody, once again be called Anti-Cartesianism.

It has been suggested already that, though Husserl in some respects seemed to adhere to the Cartesian concept of consciousness, yet, more significantly, his thought constitutes a total break with the Cartesian position. Merleau-Ponty certainly interpreted him thus, and saw himself as a direct descendant of Husserl. His first book, *The Structure of Behaviour,* published in 1938, was in fact hardly philosophical at all, though it was designed to form the foundation of philosophy. It was primarily a critique of Behaviourism, which, he argued, simply cannot be understood. In particular, he attacked the Behaviourist notion of one-to-one correlation of stimulus with response; and with this, the presupposition that causal explanations of human behaviour are possible. He did not deny that there could be found, in special laboratory conditions, a pattern of stimulus and response. He argued only that in real life, it was impossible to think of the body as a passive object, always merely reacting to external causes. We must think of it, as we normally in fact do think of it, as active, as organizing its world about it, through perception. He stated here his general aim, which he continued to pursue all the rest of his life, namely 'To understand the relations of consciousness and nature: organic, psychological or even social'.

What was wrong with the Behaviourists was that they wrongly conceived behaviour itself. Behaviour, according to Merleau-Ponty, 'Is not a material reality and not a psychical one either, but a structure which does not properly belong to the external world or to the internal life'. Behaviour in this sense is a 'manner of existing'. It is not only human beings who manifest behaviour, but they alone manifest 'symbolic forms' of behaviour. In this form of behaviour the response to a given stimulus is, as it were, mediated by rules or principles which can be deliberately chosen, and can be changed by a deliberate act of will. Thus the new concept of behaviour is that of a mode of existence which cannot be completely described in all its forms without reference to the specifically human capacity to *attribute meanings to the world*, and to consider the world in different lights (to 'transcend' given meaning).

There are several key concepts in *The Structure of Behaviour* which are taken up again in the later *Phenomenology of Perception*. The first of these is the concept of perception itself, the analysis of which is to be Merleau-Ponty's method of fulfilling his avowed aim, that of understanding the relation between consciousness and the world. Secondly, there is the concept of 'transcending' the given ('*dépassement*'). Man is able to project his intentions and his interpretations on what is physically before him, and is not committed to any *particular* projection. He is able, up to a point, to construct his own world, and his perception of this world is, therefore, always ambiguous. It is not wholly physiological nor wholly psychological; his world itself may always turn out to be different from what it seemed. One can perceive only if there is something to perceive; but *what* one perceives is not identical with, nor limited to, what is there. This is the ambiguity which is to appear in the later work as the clue to the nature of perception.

This aspect of perception and the concept of the *world of the perceiver* to which, even in perception, he is already committed, is, as I suggested in Chapter 2 an inheritance, not from the work of Husserl as a whole, but from the concept of the *Lebenswelt* which occurs only in the posthumous papers, especially those collected under the title *The Crisis in Modern Science and Transcendental Phenomenology*, of which Merleau-Ponty made a special study. But Merleau-Ponty himself did not make any great distinction between the early and the late Husserl. It is perhaps for this reason that he has frequently been accused of misinterpreting Husserl for his own ends. In fact he did not so much misinterpret, as select. His own view of phenomenology, of the significance of Husserl's work, and of his own debt to Husserl, are discussed fairly fully in the Preface to the *Phenomenology of Perception* (1945). Right at the beginning of the Preface, in his definition of phenomenology, he brings together two aspects of Husserl's thought, the 'phenomenological reduction' and the *Lebenswelt*. He says that phenomenology is

the transcendent philosophy which places in abeyance the assertions arising out of the natural attitude, the better to understand them; but it is also a philosophy for which the world is always 'already there' before reflection begins—as an inalienable presence; and all its efforts are concentrated on reachieving a direct and primitive contact with the world, and endowing that contact with a philosophical status.[1]

He admits that there is a contradiction, at first sight, between these two aims of phenomenology, namely to bracket the world, so that it is excluded from consideration, and at the same time to include it in all our analyses of thought. He says that some might wish to associate Husserl with the former and Heidegger with the latter view. But he suggests that the concept of the *Lebenswelt*, identified in the end by Husserl himself as the central theme of phenomenology, itself reconciles the contradiction, or at any rate can itself be analysed into these two separate parts.

He goes on to say that, in any case, each philosopher must find his own phenomenology for himself. He himself wishes to be called an Existentialist, and therefore one must read his work to discover

[1] *Phenomenology of Perception*, trans. C. Smith (Routledge, London, 1945), p. vii.

Existentialist Phenomenology. This is doubtless true. It is only confirmation of the proposition that one part of Existentialism, at any rate, can hardly be distinguished from Phenomenology, though this may not be exactly the phenomenology of Husserl, or of any other particular philosopher.

To return to the Preface: Merleau-Ponty insists that the most important feature of phenomenology, his or anyone's, is that it is a 'rejection of science'. Now this in itself sounds very odd, if it is thought of as a direct result of the work of Husserl, whose aim was to render philosophy wholly scientific. But the rejection of science is immediately connected with the thesis to which we shall return later, of 'the primacy of perception'. The whole of science, Merleau-Ponty says, is built upon *the world as directly experienced*.

Science has not, and never will have, by its nature, the same significance *qua* form of being as the world which we perceive, for the simple reason that it is a rationale or explanation of that world. I am, not 'a living creature', not even a 'man', not again even 'consciousness' endowed with all the characteristics which zoology, social anatomy or inductive psychology recognize in these various products of the natural or historical process—I am the absolute source, my existence does not stem from my antecedents, from my physical and social environment; instead it moves outwards towards them and sustains them, for I alone bring into being for myself (and therefore into being in the only sense the word can have for me) the tradition which I elect to carry on, or the horizon whose distance from me would be abolished—since that distance is not one of its properties—if I were not there to scan it with my gaze.[1]

This at least is obviously the pure voice of Existentialism. And though there is, as I have said before, no direct connection between Kierkegaard and Merleau-Ponty, yet at least in this passage there is more than a faint reminder of the passionate, anti-scientific, personal approach to the world which characterized Kierkegaard. 'I am the absolute source,' Kierkegaard would say of religion and ethics, Merleau-Ponty says of knowledge as a whole, because I am the source of perception.

In analysing perception he would claim, obviously, to be pursuing his general aim in philosophy, namely that of understanding the relation between consciousness and the world. In order to proceed with the analysis, it is necessary to try to discover what our normal

[1] op. cit., p. viii.

presuppositions about the world which we perceive are, and what are the perceptual foundations upon which all our knowledge is built. 'To return to the things themselves is to return to that world which precedes knowledge, of which knowledge always *speaks*.' It is very important to understand this project as precisely as possible, since the whole of the *Phenomenology of Perception* is concerned with nothing but the attempt to uncover 'the world which precedes knowledge'.

Part of the difficulty which one may have in understanding what Merleau-Ponty is doing here is that, in a way, it seems so obvious that knowledge is founded on perception, that it is hardly worth saying. *The Foundations of Empirical Knowledge,* in fact the title of a book of Ayer's, could equally well have been the title of a book by Locke, Hume, or Russell, and whichever of these philosophers had written it, we should have expected a discussion of perception to occupy most of the book.

But perception has very often been examined as a candidate for absolute certainty. It has been argued that if empirical knowledge is founded on perception, and if there actually is any empirical knowledge, then at least some perceptual judgements must be certain, otherwise they could not serve as *foundations.* The obvious weakness of ordinary perceptual judgements as candidates for certainty has led to an attempt to reformulate perceptual judgements in a way which could be clear, unambiguous, and known certainly to be true, if uttered in appropriate circumstances. So the search for foundations has led to the invention of a *properly scientific language,* which could, in theory, be used for the recording of perceptions. The point of such a language is always to stick to what is perceived, not go beyond what is actually given, to speak of *sense-data,* not objects, and to attempt, as far as possible, to refer to a particular moment in time, the moment of the perception.

No one who discussed such a theoretical language would claim that it could be used instead of ordinary language; certainly no one would claim that in making ordinary statements about the world we were translating from a sense-datum language into an ordinary object-language. There is no sense in saying that such a language 'precedes' the ordinary language in which our ordinary knowledge is expressed. The very most that would be claimed is that, unless such a language were possible to construct, there could be no such thing as knowledge.

Merleau-Ponty's aim in describing perception is utterly different from this familiar Anglo-Saxon aim. He is not particularly concerned with *certainty*. His argument is not, 'If science is to be certain then we must show how perception can be certain, since science is founded on perception.' He says rather that even science is bounded by the limits of the scientist. Science, and knowledge in general, is one, somewhat formalized, relation between a conscious being and the world. But before anything arose which could be called either knowledge or science, there was already a much more basic, less rational, connection between the conscious being and the world, namely perception. It is literally true that perception *precedes* knowledge. A baby has perception and no knowledge. It is even possible to conceive of a primitive race of men, or near-men, who had perception and no knowledge. There is a sense, indeed, in which Merleau-Ponty's undertaking is more historical than logical. When he wishes to analyse perception, then, he is not concerned with how we may *express* our perceptual judgements; he is not concerned with how we could render such judgements infallible. He is not concerned with judgements at all, but, as far as possible, with perception itself, with what it is like to perceive. His undertaking is first and foremost descriptive. It is, of course, not at all easy to describe perception and to keep it separate from scientific knowledge, or, worse still, from language. But it is this which he is attempting.

It is here that he uses the technique of the '*epoché*', the setting the world in brackets. In the description of this pre-knowledge perception which is his concern, the greatest danger to avoid is the taking over, not of any particular piece of scientific knowledge, but of the whole scientific assumption that the world consists of objects, which are completely and totally distinct from the observing subject. It is in the effort to avoid this danger that Merleau-Ponty makes use of the concept of the *Lebenswelt*, and of his own, often obscure, doctrine of the relation between the subject and the world, the nature of which it is his whole aim to clarify.

In the Preface itself he sketches his final doctrine:

The world is not an object such that I have in my possession the law of its making; it is the natural setting and the field for all my thoughts and all my explicit perceptions. Truth does not inhabit only the 'inner man', or, more accurately, there is no inner man; man is in the world and only in the world does he know himself. When I return to myself from an excursion into the realm of dogmatic common sense or of science, I find, not a source of intrinsic truth, but a subject destined to be in the world.[1]

This particular passage from the Preface is, as will be easily seen, somewhat rhetorical in tone. It contains, as rhetoric often does, some rather shaky transitions of thought. There is, for example, no real opposition, such as is implied in the passage quoted, between there being an 'inner man' and man's being 'in the world'. Common sense, which is castigated along with science as that which supposes objects to exist distinct from the observing subject, might well hold both that men are 'in the world' and that there is an 'inner man' (that there is the possibility of reflective consciousness, of man thinking *that* he is a thinking being). However, as is often true both of Merleau-Ponty and of Sartre, though the argument may be faulty, the meaning is clear. The theme of the *Phenomenology of Perception* is that, to understand man's place in the world, we must understand perception, and that we cannot understand perception as long as we insist upon an absolute distinction between the perceiving subject and the object perceived. Science is thrown out just because it does make this distinction, and so is 'dogmatic common sense'. At the end of the Preface Merleau-Ponty sums up the non-scientific view as follows: 'Because we are in the world, we are *condemned to meaning*.' We must now try to see where this Husserl-inspired theory of our relation with the world leads him in the ensuing pages.

There is a sense in which the *Phenomenology of Perception* is a disappointing book, especially to English-speaking readers. The Preface promises much. The subject-matter, perception itself, is familiar and interesting, the criticisms of Hume and Descartes are illuminating, though oddly undocumented for our taste. But the positive thesis of the book seems sadly thin, when one gets to it. Engagement in the world is repeatedly emphasized as the clue to the understanding of perception, but it is hard not to feel that, this being said, there is little else which enhances our understanding. All the same the book, despite all its repetitions, is enjoyable to read, largely because its method appears so empirical.

It will be remembered that the aim is not to discuss language, but on the contrary to expose to view what we all know perfectly

[1] op. cit., p. xi.

well, in some sense, namely what perceiving *is*: what it is like to perceive things. The chief way of doing this is to take the case of someone whose perception is abnormal and defective, in order to see, by contrast, what normal perception is like. This is an excellent and fascinating method.

The patient (Schneider) whose case is considered in the *Phenomenology of Perception* was suffering, as the result of an injury, from visual and motor defects. His case was originally written up and discussed by the psychologists Gelb and Goldstein,[1] and later by Goldstein alone. A great number of extracts from the case history is employed by Merleau-Ponty, of which I shall quote just one:

If a fountain pen is shown to the patient, in such a way that the clip is not seen, the phases of recognition are as follows. 'It is black, blue and shiny,' says the patient. 'There is a white patch on it, and it is rather long; it is the shape of a stick. It may be some sort of instrument . . .' The pen is then brought closer, and the clip is turned towards the patient. He goes on, 'It must be a pencil or a fountain pen' (he touches his breast pocket). 'It is put there to make notes with.' It is clear that language intervenes at every stage of recognition by providing possible meanings for what is in fact seen, and that recognition advances *pari passu* with linguistic connections: from 'long' to 'shaped like a stick', from 'stick' to 'instrument' and from there to 'instrument for noting things down', and finally to 'fountain pen'. The sense data are limited to suggesting these meanings as a fact suggests an hypothesis to the physicist. . . .

Merleau-Ponty then goes on to draw the contrast between this and the normal perceptual case.

This procedure . . . throws into relief the spontaneous method of normal perception, that kind of living system of meanings which makes the concrete essence of the object immediately recognizable and allows its 'sensible properties' to appear only through that essence. It is this familiarity and communication with the object which is here interrupted. In the normal subject the object 'speaks' and is significant, the arrangement of colours straightway 'means' something, whereas in Schneider, the meaning has to be brought in from elsewhere by a veritable act of interpretation. Conversely in the normal person the subject's intentions are immediately reflected in the perceptual field,

[1] *Uber den Einfluss des vollstandigen Verlustes des optisches Vorstellungsvermogens auf das tactile Erkennen Psychologische Analysen hirnpathologischer Falle*, Chapter II.

polarizing it or placing their seal upon it, or setting up in it, effort-
lessly, a wave of significance. In the patient the perceptual field has lost
this plasticity.[1]

It is clear from this passage that Schneider's kind of perception is
very much more like the way that a phenomenalist or sense-datum
philosopher might imagine perception, if perception followed its
logical course. (Once again, one should remember that sense-datum
philosophers did not suppose that perception *was* like this; they
were interested in the language of perception, not its occurrence in
fact. But if, logically, one's perceptual statements are 'built up'
out of sense-data statements, then it is at least possible to imagine
how it would be to 'build-up' one's perception of something as a
fountain pen from basic data such as 'longish black, shiny', etc.)
In contrast to this, Merleau-Ponty describes the normal case, where
an object is immediately an object-with-significance-for-us. This is
the way in which we are 'condemned to things'.

We can tell that proper perception consists of significant perception, because we can recognize as abnormal a kind of perception stripped of meanings, or where meanings have to be
laboriously built up.

In attacking the 'visual sphere', illness is not limited to destroying
certain contents of consciousness, visual representations, or sight,
literally speaking; it affects sight in the figurative sense, of which the
former is no more than the model or symbol . . . a certain way of positing
the object, or being aware.[2]

But Schneider's defects were of the motor powers as well as
visual, and this is important. For it is, according to Merleau-Ponty,
through the ability to move our own limbs that we attach significance to our world. He somewhat mysteriously quotes Husserl as
having said 'Consciousness is in the first place not a matter of "I
think that" but of "I can".' (This is mysterious in that no one seems
able exactly to trace this quotation, which may be a recollection of
a lecture, or a misquotation.) Sight and movement are both of them
ways of entering into relationship with the world.

Objects exist for us as they are, for instance, 'in our way', 'able to
support us', 'out of reach', 'suitable for use as a lever' and so on.
All such concepts as these depend on our own instinctive knowledge not of the objects themselves so much as of our own bodies,

[1] op. cit., pp. 131 f.   [2] op. cit., p. 136.

our size, our mobility, the length of our reach, and so on. Things in the world are potential tools, and the notion of a tool essentially depends on a notion of our own physical characteristics, and our position in space. This awareness of our own bodies looks like just that kind of pre-knowledge relation to the world which Merleau-Ponty is committed to discovering.

But there seems to be a considerable confusion between different kinds of knowledge in his examples, and by no means all of them are, in the way he would like to argue, pre-rational, or basic to our perception of the world.

First he speaks of our knowledge of the actual position of our limbs. This has also been discussed (in connection, and by way of analogy, with our knowledge of our own intentions) by Elizabeth Anscombe, under the description 'knowledge without observation'. It does indeed seem that we have a kind of basic awareness, at a perceptual level, of the position (though not necessarily of the location) of our own limbs. But, besides this, Merleau-Ponty discusses a number of different kinds of knowledge, which he appears to think of as exactly the same. For example, he notes that if one has an extension to one's body (for example a tall feather on one's hat) one may become adept at knowing how to get through doors without catching the feather on the top of the door. Or if one is accustomed to driving a particular car, one may feel as if the car is 'an extension of oneself' so that one knows whether or not one can get through a certain space. But the difficulty here is that in fact one may, and sometimes does, get it wrong. And one is very likely to hit the feather on one's hat the first time one wears it. Moreover, even where the question is not about a putative extension of one's body itself, it is still not *always* intuitively certain whether or not one can, for example, get through a certain gap, reach a particular branch, or anything else of the kind. Of course we are very good at solving the most common problems of this kind, which indeed scarcely seem like problems. But there are rare or difficult cases where plainly we have to *guess* whether we can do something, and find out whether we can or not by trying. If this is so, then the kind of knowledge which we have when we know for certain that we *can* do something, is knowledge by experience. It is obviously dependent on perception, but it would be wrong to say that it *was* perception, since we may actually, in some cases, discover the stages by which we see, guess, try, and perhaps fail.

That sometimes a car may be an extension of oneself (so that for example if you say to me in my car, 'Go back to the corner', I can obey as easily and with as little thought as if you had said to me on foot, 'Go back to the corner') does not entail that the world is mediated through my body and its extension in a way which 'precedes knowledge'. It shows only that we acquire skills and habits by long practice. Merleau-Ponty has an example of an organist who can learn the positions of the stops of a new organ in a few minutes, and then play as well as on an organ he is used to. This is supposed to show that the really good organist *takes on* any organ, and uses it, as he uses his own body, to express the music he is playing. But in fact it shows nothing more than that an experienced organist can play any organ, as an experienced driver can drive any car, because far the most important things about playing the organ or driving a car are common to all cases. It is not tremendously important where the stops are or how many there are. If you can play the organ, you can extrapolate from one instrument to another, and this is because, basically, organs are alike. This kind of knowledge acquired through practice seems, when one looks into it, to have nothing whatever to do with the knowledge we have of our own bodies, that is, of where our limbs are.

A different kind of knowledge still is discussed by Merleau-Ponty in the same context. This is non-verbalized knowledge of various sorts. The knowledge that we may have of how to avoid a certain beam, or how to get from one room to another in a familiar house in the dark, is not verbalized and probably could not be. And obviously there are many far more complicated skills, in the exercise of which we cannot explain verbally what we are doing. It may be practically impossible for a typist to say what order the letters on a typewriter come in, or for an experienced player to reconstruct verbally the fingering of a scale on a musical instrument. But, once again, the fact that we cannot describe in words what we do does not entail a 'pre-knowledge' relation between our bodies and the world. It entails only that we may learn *how to do* things as well as learning *that certain things* are the case. If all that Merleau-Ponty is doing is telling us that there is knowing how, as well as knowing that, then we shall not dispute it. But he seems to be arguing for a far more momentous thesis in this part of the book, namely that the basic element in the nature of perception is our perception of the world as 'the environment of our bodies'; and that this kind of relation to the world is actually prior to knowledge, not in logic but in fact. It is not that I wish to deny that there is truth in his account of perception. It is only that, in the particular range of arguments about the body, he seems to me to have confused too many different kinds of knowledge—learning, habit-acquiring, skill-using, and so on—for any very precise conclusion to follow.

However the general conclusion is clear: 'Our own body is in the world as the heart is in the organism: it keeps the visible spectacle constantly alive.' This connection of the world with ourselves through our bodies is what gives meaning to the world. The world is 'kept constantly alive' by being constantly endowed with significance to us. Once again, it is probably better to speak of 'significance' rather than 'meaning', just because 'meaning' suggests something precise and even systematic, while 'significance' does not. Very small portions of our experienced world are systematic. Most of what we perceive is interesting, hostile, frightening, charming, and so on, and all these characteristics could be covered by the term 'significance' without difficulty. The significance enters through our body because it is with our bodies, our hands or our limbs or our tools, that we will intervene in the world, if we do. If we see an object as frightening, this is to see it as something *from which we are prepared actually to run away*. In seeing something as threatening, we may at the same time raise our arm to fend it off. Seeing it, seeing it as significant, and seeing it as to-be-fended-off are all the same thing, and are all true perception.

Merleau-Ponty has curiously little to say about mistaken perception which, on his view of perception itself, should be an interesting and somewhat complex subject. There would presumably be some cases where I am mistaken about my own body, and some where I am mistaken about the feature in the world which relates to my body (as I might wrongly suppose that something was solid enough to bear me when it was not, either because I am heavier than I thought, or because the surface of the object is misleading as to its solidity). But it is not clear that Merleau-Ponty would admit this distinction. The trouble is that to admit this double way of possibly being wrong would be to admit that our 'knowledge' of what we can do is not always knowledge at all but often guesswork, as I have already suggested.

But, though he says little about normally mistaken perceptions, Merleau-Ponty has an interesting discussion of hallucinations, towards the end of the *Phenomenology of Perception*. 'Hallucination', he says, 'causes the real to disintegrate before our eyes, and puts a quasi-reality in its place, and in both these respects this phenomenon brings us back to the prelogical basis of our knowledge.' It is an agreeable change for readers brought up on the somewhat sparse illustrations of hallucination discussed in, for instance, G. E. Moore (who discusses 'Macbeth's dagger') or A. J. Ayer (who, absurdly, classes mirages as hallucinations) to be presented with a few genuine examples drawn from psychiatric casebooks, with, very often, the patient's own description of the hallucination to help him understand it. The main purpose of the illustrations is to show that the patient himself distinguishes quite clearly between his hallucinatory experience and real experience. 'The subject who, in delirium tremens, takes the doctor's hand to be a guinea-pig, is immediately aware of the fact when a real guinea-pig is placed in his other hand.'

The fact that in this and other cases there is an obvious qualitative difference between the real and the hallucinatory experience is taken by Merleau-Ponty to show that neither an 'empiricist' nor an 'intellectualist' account of hallucination will do. The empiricist is supposed to treat hallucinatory experience as sense-contents, simply caused in some manner other than the normal manner. The sense-data are supposed by the empiricist to be *qualitatively* indistinguishable from normal sense-data. They just possess certain extra, odd, features to distinguish them from the normal, such as not being available to other people, and perhaps not being capable of verification by the evidence of another sense than the sense first employed (for instance, an hallucinatory voice proceeds from no *visible* source). The intellectualist alleges that an hallucination is a false belief: that it is, for instance, the false belief that I am seeing something, when in fact I am not; or the false belief that the doctor's hand is a guinea-pig. But if it is true, as all the evidence suggests, that the patient in some sense does *not* believe that he sees when he does not, or does not really *believe* the doctor's hand to be a guinea-pig, then this account will have to be rejected as well. So far Merleau-Ponty's discussion is interesting and convincing, as long as it is entirely critical. But, as so often happens in this book, when it comes to replacing the rejected accounts of hallucination with a positive account of his own, we are all over again bombarded with rhetoric, and what emerges is simply one more statement, very likely true, that the perceiving subject is, in hallucination, in some basically odd relation to the external world.

The patient is interested not in the 'objective world' but in what strikes him, what affects him. The value which most of us attach to reality is attached by the patient to a myth, which is significant for him alone. But his case is not utterly different from our own, since we all of us, in perceiving the world, attach our own value to it; and the supreme myth, as we have already seen, is that there is such a thing as perfectly objective reality.

The patient's existence is displaced from its centre, being no longer enacted through dealings with a harsh resistant and intractable world which has no knowledge of us, but expending its substance in isolation, creating a fictitious setting for itself. But this fiction can have the value of reality only because, in the normal subject, reality itself suffers through an analogous process.

Hallucination would not be possible unless there were the possibility for all of us, all the time, of misinterpreting or distorting the world in perception. Perception is always ambiguous, partly subjective, partly 'transcendental', going beyond the immediate present, into a future where what I perceive will remain an object or a tool. It is the fact of this ambiguity which makes it possible to suffer from illusions or hallucinations.

It is the pure Cartesian subject, receiving into his limpid consciousness unadulterated messages from the objective, stable outside world, who is here, as elsewhere, under attack. A subject's consciousness is not 'pure', because it is inevitably attached to his own body, which *is* his contact with the world; the outside world is not pure because it is always only an object *for* one person, and therefore perceived by him from his own point of view, and coloured by his own preconceptions, desires and fears. If we have this kind of understanding of ourselves, as the subject of perception, not isolated, but in the world, and moreover in *our own* world, then the next question is, how are we to understand other subjects? 'How can the word "I" be put into the plural?' Merleau-Ponty's answer to this question is extraordinarily simple. 'If I experience this inhering of my consciousness in my body and its world, the perception of other people and the plurality of consciousnesses no longer present any difficulty. . . . If my consciousness has a body, why should not other bodies "have" consciousness?' In other words there are other bodies in my world, and they cannot be conceptually detached from consciousness any more than I can, in my own case, conceptually detach 'mind' from 'body'. The destruction of the Cartesian myth carries with it the destruction of solipsism.

Merleau-Ponty denies that this is the old argument by analogy for the existence of other people (the argument according to which, seeing people's bodies or their hats and umbrellas, one was supposed to argue that they contained minds like our own). There cannot be an argument of analogy involved, Merleau-Ponty suggests, since I recognize the behaviour of other people and understand it *before* I have learned in my own case to correlate bodily movements with thoughts or intentions. 'A baby can imitate a grown-up's behaviour, long before he has any separate concept of his own behaviour.' 'It (the baby) perceives its intentions in its own body, and my body with its own, and thereby my intentions in its own body.' The notion of human *behaviour* is the operative thing here. I immediately interpret the acts of another human body as 'behaviour' and this is, of its nature, intelligible only in terms of intersubjective significance. 'No sooner has my gaze fallen upon a living body in the process of acting, than the objects surrounding it immediately take on a fresh layer of significance: they are no longer simply what I could make of them, they are what this other pattern of behaviour is about to make of them.' All this comes about the more easily because of the existence of language, which is designed to make explicit and formal the significance which things have, not for one person alone, but for one person *among others*.

To understand one's relation to the world, then, means, among other things, to understand one's relation to other people. Philosophy must be largely social philosophy. It is on this note that the second part of the *Phenomenology of Perception* ends. Merleau-Ponty has by now exposed the traditional prejudices about perception, given his account first of the subject, and then of the world, the object. The third part of the book is a final and rather brief account of how subject and object are brought together, and of the true relationship between them (though naturally much of this ground has been covered already earlier in the book).

The third part is divided into three chapters, one on the *Cogito*, the second on Temporality and the last on Freedom. The prose style of the book at this stage becomes very turgid indeed, full of paradoxes and oracular utterances. It is no longer easy to bring any exactitude to the analysis of the text through the help of the examples, since there are almost none. But the main conclusion both of the chapter on the *Cogito* and of that on Temporality is the same, and is not different from the conclusion of the book as a whole.

The sense of '*cogito*' in which Merleau-Ponty is interested is that of a kind of vestigial self-consciousness (what Sartre, as we shall see, refers to as the 'pre-reflective *cogito*') which accompanies all my actions and thoughts, all my understanding of the significance of the world. This consciousness is inseparable from my body and is grounded, as all knowledge is, in perception. In perception I have this consciousness; but unlike Descartes's '*cogito*' it is not supposed to give rise to any propositions which are indubitable, indeed it cannot be said to give rise to any *propositions* at all. For propositions require language, and this vestigial consciousness of myself, which is, Merleau-Ponty says, identical with my existence, is *before* language. In learning language, I already have this consciousness, so that I am able to distinguish myself from the world, and to pick up the idea of which part of the world the word that I am learning applies to. For example, in learning to use the word 'hail', a child suddenly finds himself applying it one day, and applying it correctly, to what is falling from the sky. The precondition of his doing this is his already existent perception of the world and therefore awareness of himself, as the observer and the describer of the world. There could be no purely intellectual self-consciousness, since self-consciousness goes with perception, which is dependent on my being my body. Thus Descartes's doubts about his own body, which were a part of his doubt about the existence of the external world, are argued by Merleau-Ponty to be absolutely meaningless; for without the body there would be no '*cogito*' at all.

Now since a body is a particular spatial object, occupying a certain position in space, all perception and all awareness is from a certain spatial point, and refers to other points in space. In the same way, perception is also necessarily perception at a particular time, and it refers to time past and time to come. Without the continuity of the body in time, the subject could not make any sense of the world he observed.

At this point in his argument, Merleau-Ponty borrows very literally from Heidegger. His thesis is that, from the standpoint of science, there could be no such thing as time. Science is supposed to be concerned with objective observable facts, what is the case here and now; since the future does not yet exist and the past does not exist any longer, future and past events cannot strictly be the concern of science. The objective world cannot be more than a series of present events, 'only so many instances of "now"'. In order to make sense of these, the idea of continuity, that is, the idea of time, must be introduced, and to introduce this is immediately to introduce subjectivity. This is because time just is a part of my immediate experience, in the same way as space is. 'A past and a future spring forth only when I reach out for them.' 'The passage of one present to the next is not something which I conceive, nor do I see it as an onlooker, I perform it.' I make my world's tempo in making it intelligible and useable.

Thus both consciousness of self, in a minimal sense, and consciousness of time, are absolutely essential to our existence in the world, as beings who can perceive and who can act. Merleau-Ponty next uses the concept of time as a way of introducing his final topic, that of freedom. But it is at this point also that the idea of other people, of social philosophy, is reintroduced. Freedom is the possibility of action and this in itself presupposes time, as we have seen. But, unlike space, a *single time* is supposed to be capable of containing more than one person The idea of 'now' does not exclude the same 'now' being, as it were, occupied by more persons than one, as the idea of 'here' strictly interpreted seems to.

Merleau-Ponty introduces the discussion of freedom in the last chapter of the book by rejecting the view that there could be a *causal* connection between my actions and the world. For one thing to cause another they must be thought of as two separate things or events. The burning match, for example, causes the forest fire, the earthquake causes the collapse of the building. In each case there are two separable elements in the causal judgement. Merleau-Ponty's argument seems to be that my action cannot be caused by the physical world, since the relation between me and the world is too close. It and I are one. It is not that I am the subject and the world the separate object. Hence, if my actions are not caused by the world, they are free. And if any of them is free then, at least in some sense, all of them are free.

The limitations upon my freedom which undoubtedly exist only, in fact, confirm that I am free, since it is I who see them as limitations or obstacles. And the concept of an obstacle, in general, could arise only for a being who was free and who therefore could do some things and aspire but fail to do others. An obstacle could not exist except as an obstacle to a free will.

Now as I know that I am free, then apparently I know also that other people are free because, Merleau-Ponty boldly states, in knowing myself, I know others at the same time. 'I must . . . in the most radical reflection apprehend around my individuality a kind of halo of generality or a kind of atmosphere of sociality.' It is because I am aware of 'sociality' in being aware of myself that I am able to apply to myself public labels which I know already as applying to others. For instance one can learn to classify the feelings of which one is aware in oneself as 'jealousy' or 'boredom', and one can learn to classify oneself along with other people as 'bourgeois' or 'intellectual'. It is from precisely such classifications that historical changes, revolutions, and reforms have their origins. Exploitation, Merleau-Ponty says, existed long before revolution. Revolution came only when the proletariat learned to identify themselves as such. We shall find this idea more fully examined in Sartre.

Merleau-Ponty has two notions here which may seem to be incompatible: the first, that man is totally free; the second, that he is totally a part of his physical and social environment and can do and be nothing except in so far as he realizes that he is part of that environment. It looks as though the second notion comes very near to determinism. We must see how he attempts to reconcile these conflicting views.

First, although he has said that man is totally free, he now, halfway through the discussion, denies that a man 'chooses himself' from the beginning with nothing to determine him at all. A man is not *just* consciousness and the possibility of action. If he were, then he might really be said to choose himself. But as we have repeatedly been told, he is in fact deeply embedded in the real world, and he has commitments, pre-suppositions, attitudes, and habits from which he cannot disengage himself at will. So what does his freedom amount to? Merleau-Ponty's answer, though portentous, is not very clear.

Freedom is ambiguity; it is indeed an aspect of that ambiguity which first made its appearance in the early *Structure of Behaviour*. There the ambiguity arose from the fact that though I can perceive only what is before me, yet in perceiving I have gone beyond what is actually before me. Likewise, in action, I go beyond what I would do (have to do) if I were totally committed, or totally determined by my environment. I see ahead as I would not if I were thing-like or mechanical. But when I have initiated a course of action, once again I am, as it were, carried along by what I have started, so that at any moment I may seem either committed or free. 'The generality of the role and of the situation comes to the aid of decision, and in this exchange between the situation and the person who takes it up, it is impossible to determine precisely the "share contributed by the situation" and the "share contributed by freedom".'[1] In my world, surrounded as I am by people, supported by their expectations and their descriptions of me, I am free to pursue projects for the future, because I am capable of reflecting on past and future alike. A 'pure' consciousness would be concerned with the present alone, and would thus have no possibility of acting.

By the end of Merleau-Ponty's last chapter, consciousness, temporality, sociality, and freedom all come together in some manner which is less than entailment, but is perhaps slightly more than mere rhetorical association. The name of this association is 'my being in the world'. Husserl's *Lebenswelt* and Heidegger's *Dasein* are both here together in the last pages of the *Phenomenology of Perception*.

After the publication of this book, Merleau-Ponty gave a lecture to the Societé Française de Philosophie entitled *The Primacy of Perception* which was a kind of summary and defence of his major work. For the most part the lecture does simply summarize, emphasizing the thesis that perception is our connection with the world, even with the world of science, and that this connection is not the relationship between pure subject and pure object, but between a man who is a part of the world, and that world of which he is a part. 'By these words the "primacy of perception" we mean that the experience of perception is our presence at the moment when things, truths, values are constituted for us, that perception is a

[1] op. cit., p. 453.

nascent *logos*; that it teaches us outside all dogmatism, the true conditions of objectivity itself; that it summons us to the tasks of knowledge and action.' He goes on to say that The *Phenomenology of Perception* is only an introduction to the subject. In particular, it remains to apply the method employed in that book to culture and history. He also suggests that in doing this, consequences for morals will become clear.

It is easy to see the commitment, the involvement, and the practicality of Existentialism in these words. The nature of subjectivity and of human freedom, these truly Existentialist topics, are not worked out here in their practical consequences, but there is at least a hint as to how it might be done, and an absolute statement that it should be done. In fact, though his unfinished last work, *The Visible and the Invisible*, seems to have left the specifically human sphere for the dubious territory of Being itself, it is hard to believe that even here he would have completely lost faith in the ultimately explanatory nature of perception, the investigation and description of which was to show the way in which the individual man was exposed to the world in which he found himself.

5
Jean-Paul Sartre (1)

We have now seen how Merleau-Ponty derived the great Existentialist concepts, Freedom and Individuality or Subjectivity, from the consideration of man's connection with the world in perception. The relation between one man and another was also considered, but only as a part of the general examination of man's relation with his world.

When we turn our attention now to Sartre, his older but still living contemporary, we shall find a new emphasis, but the same themes. However, the structure of his main Existentialist book, *Being and Nothingness*, is complex, and though I shall attempt to deal first with his analysis of the world of objects and then with the world of other people, it will be found that this division cannot be clear-cut. For the concepts of Nothingness and of Freedom are essential to both parts, and indeed form the recurring theme of the whole book. Moreover all the ideas explored in the book interlock in more than one way.

I shall try, first, to clarify Sartre's use of the concept of nothingness, and his related distinction between man and the world of concrete non-conscious things. In the next chapter I shall be concerned with the relations between men and each other, as cohabiters of the world; with Sartre's implied ethical views; and with the final disintegration, in his hands, of Existentialist philosophy (though this last can be dealt with only briefly). For the most part I shall try to expound only the views formulated in *Being and Nothingness*, though it will be necessary to say something about Sartre's later book, *The Critique of Dialectical Reason*, in the next chapter. The earlier works on the imagination and the emotions will not be discussed at all, although it was through them that Sartre first introduced the philosophy of Husserl to France.

The title of Sartre's great Existentialist book, *Being and Nothingness*, might raise doubts about the propriety of calling him an Existentialist at all. For it was precisely on the grounds that he was interested in Being in general that Heidegger rejected the title Existentialism for his own philosophy. But, though Sartre, in the title and in the book itself, proposes to examine the notion of Being, he does so from a purely human position; that is, he is primarily interested in *human* existence; and Being in general is introduced only as that within which the crucial distinction between human and other existence is drawn.

We must start, in any case, not with Being, but with nothingness, for the idea of nothingness is central to Sartre's Existentialism. It will be remembered that in the chapter on Heidegger, two senses of the word 'Nothingness' were introduced. In the first sense, nothingness was a kind of gap or separation which lay between a man and the world, or rather between a man's consciousness and the world of objects of which he was conscious. The second sense of 'Nothingness' was that almost of 'futility', of the vanishing and evaporating of objects in the world. Without an awareness of nothingness in this sense, a man could not begin to move from inauthentic to authentic existence. If these two senses can be characterized as the epistemological and the emotional, then it would be true to say that Sartre made use mainly of the epistemological sense of the word. Sartre, as we shall see, insists that a man in the world must adopt *some* emotional attitude towards it, but it is not, in his case, the sense of nothingness which determines how he feels.

In other than emotional respects, however, it is impossible for Sartre to account for the relation between man and the world without employing the concept of nothingness. Man, a conscious being, is distinguished as a 'Being-for-itself' from unconscious objects, which are 'Beings-in-themselves'. (There is also a third manner of being, though not a third kind of object, namely 'Being-for-others', but the discussion of this will be deferred until the next chapter.) Naturally, as we saw in Heidegger's philosophy, the most important feature which marks off conscious from other beings is their ability to *consider the world* in which they find themselves, and to think of themselves as separate from other things. Their consciousness is therefore referred to as the gap or space, the emptiness which divides them from Beings-in-themselves. In this aspect, nothingness is like space; it is outside the conscious being, and it constitutes the distance which divides him from his world. In another aspect, nothingness is thought of as internal to the Being-for-itself. It is the emptiness *within* him which he aims to fill by his own actions, his thoughts and his perceptions. It is the possession of this emptiness in himself which makes it possible for a Being-for-itself both to perceive the world and also to act in it, determining his own course of action by reference to an imagined future. His freedom is defined in terms of his own potentiality. For Sartre, as for Heidegger, a human being is a being with unrealized potential; whereas a Being-in-itself is solid, *massif*, entirely actual. Its future is completely determined by the fact that it is, let us say, an ink-well, or a ball. A human being has no essence (his 'Existence precedes his Essence'); he is therefore not wholly determined, but is free to fill the internal gap in his nature in whatever way he chooses.

In this sense, therefore, the nothingness of human nature is, paradoxically, its most important feature. In both aspects, the external and the internal, a conscious being is aware, through nothingness, of the *difference* between himself and his world; and thus a percipient human being will always be aware, in however vestigial a way, of himself as perceiving. Whether the object of his perception is the external world or some aspect of himself, still, going along with the first-order awareness, there will be a second-order awareness, of himself being aware. This is, according to Sartre, an essential and defining characteristic of consciousness itself, and he refers to it as the 'pre-reflective *cogito*', rightly or wrongly associating it with Descartes's theory that we have a direct and certain knowledge of the mind, as opposed to the body. It will be clear how much, at this point, is shared by Sartre and Merleau-Ponty.

There is yet another aspect of the concept of nothingness, where Sartre departs from the doctrine of Heidegger. We have noticed that, although it is tempting to identify Heidegger's concept with the idea of negation, he himself refused to accept a connection between 'Nothingness' and 'Negation'. Sartre, on the other hand, quite readily connects the two ideas. Negation forms the subject matter, indeed, of Part I of *Being and Nothingness*. It is first defined in terms of man's proneness to ask questions, and therefore to be ready for a negative as well as for an affirmative reply to his question. Moreover, Sartre wants to insist that people come across the idea of Not-being, or Not-being-such-and-such, in two ways. First, they encounter it in their thought about the world, and their classification of it; for, after all, one cannot attempt the most rudimentary classifications without thinking that, for instance, evergreen trees are those which are *not* deciduous. But generally people actually experience not-being directly, in their perception of the world.

Sartre describes a situation in which I go into a café, expecting to see a friend, Pierre, and discover by perception, and immediately, that he is not there. The café and all the other people fall immediately into a background, against which I expect to see Pierre stand out. But he does not. 'I witness the successive disappearance of all the objects before my eyes, particularly the faces, which hold my attention for a moment (Is that Pierre?) then immediately disintegrate just because they "are not" Pierre's face. . . . What is apparent to the intuition is a fluttering movement of non-existence, the non-existence of the background whose nihilization calls for the existence of a form, and of the form itself, a non-existence, gliding like no-thing over the surface of the background.' Of course many other people besides Pierre are *not* in the café at any particular moment. But that they are not is something which I may *think*, rather than perceive. The absence of someone whom I had expected to see is a *perceived* absence, an actual experienced negation or nothingness, which simply, by its clarity, illuminates the general fact that negation can and does enter our perceptual experience of the world.

Having thus, in a highly characteristic and concrete way, established the fact that we are all of us aware of nothingness and of negation in the word, Sartre goes on to introduce a most important connected concept, that of Bad Faith. It is very difficult to make out absolutely clearly, here or elsewhere in Sartre's work, in which direction his argument is moving. He appears very often to introduce two closely related concepts and argue both from the admitted existence of the one to the inferred existence of the other, and also the other way round. But this is perhaps not either as confusing or as surprising as it might be, since in the end, time and again, he tries to produce, as a final proof that things are as he says they are, a concrete empirical example. It is, indeed, this ultimate appeal to the particular and the concrete which has come to be thought of as the distinguishing characteristic of Existentialist philosophy as a whole. The course of the discussion of Bad Faith, then, is not only of interest in itself but is also a useful and central example of Sartre's philosophical method. For time and again, to reinforce and sometimes to replace genuine argument, Sartre attempts to get his readers to realize what reality is actually like by means of an anecdote, or verbal picture. It is the *quality* of life, not its bare description, with which he is concerned.

He objects, for example, to the whole idea of the phenomenological '*epoché*', the putting of the world inside brackets, and this in spite of his great admiration for the work of Husserl, so far as it is purely psychological. For, he argues, things in the world just will not submit to being bracketed. They exist, fully, and as obstacles to ourselves. It is of no use to try to isolate the 'pure contents of Consciousness'. There is no such thing. He goes further, that is to say, than Merleau-Ponty, in aiming at *Existential* Phenomenology, namely at a phenomenology which is concerned with real existence in the world, and his interest in true phenomenology as practised by Husserl had almost withered away by the time he came to write *Being and Nothingness*. It may well seem that Sartre's objection to Husserl is rather like Dr. Johnson's refutation of Berkeley's idealism, the refutation by kicking a stone. And the comparison would not be altogether unfair. Sartre is saying that previous philosophers have failed to give a convincing account of the world, simply through neglecting to consider *what it is like* being in the world. The *realité Vécue* is what he himself attempts to present, philosophically.

He, like Merleau-Ponty, is concerned to answer the question how we are to describe the interaction between man and the world, between Beings-for-themselves and Beings-in-themselves. And in the attempt to answer this question he argues both from certain very general features of the world which he assumes to exist (such as this very distinction between Things-for-themselves and Things-in-themselves) to the particular nature of individual situations in the world; and also, starting from a description of a particular scene, he argues that this could not be a true description, which we recognize that it is, unless in general the world were as he wishes to say it is. In this pattern of argument, he starts from observations, often of an acute and illuminating kind, of how people in fact behave, and argues that they could not behave in this way unless the whole structure of the world were thus and so.

In both kinds of argument a great difficulty has been thought to arise. For if people are committed by the structure of the world to the kind of behaviour which he describes, then what becomes of their freedom, that characteristic which is supposed to distinguish them from mere inanimate Beings-in-themselves? The difficulty may be expressed in this way: If the anecdotes which Sartre relates (for instance, about Bad Faith) are illuminating, as they are; if they bring to life a particular kind of human behaviour, practised by a particular, recognizable *kind* of person, then it cannot be right to ascribe this kind of behaviour to *everyone*, all the time and necessarily. If we are all guilty of Bad Faith all the time, then Bad Faith ceases to be an interesting accusation to bring against any individual; indeed it ceases to be an accusation at all.

But perhaps this is not so real a difficulty as it seems. For Sartre is arguing from the *possibility* of Bad Faith to the existence of a human consciousness, compounded partly of Nothingness, and he shows that Bad Faith is *possible* by showing that in some cases it is actual. Again, he argues from the most general features of consciousness to the particular *possibility* of Bad Faith, not its necessary existence in all cases.

Taking first, then, the argument from the general to the particular, Sartre proceeds as follows: there are certain features of Beings-for-themselves from which it is possible to derive the concrete fact of Bad Faith. As we have seen, Beings-for-themselves are necessarily conscious of themselves at least in a vestigial, pre-reflective way; and they are thereby also conscious that they are different from other people and other things. The power to say to oneself 'I am not such-and-such' is the experienced effect which the vacancy or gap within consciousness produces. The internal nothingness actually is, as we have seen, what constitutes consciousness. Without it, a man would be a solid *massif* thing incapable of perception or self-determination. Though Sartre does not explicitly say so, it seems that he is identifying conscious beings with language-using beings. For it is in the ability to formulate categories by which one thing is distinguished from another that the nothingness which is negation emerges; and this category-formation is, obviously, crucially connected with the use of language. Animals would be dubiously conscious, in Sartre's use of the term, and this is absurd. But if we explicitly identified a Being-for-itself with a user of language, then we could say that an animal, though conscious, was not a For-itself. According to this classification, consciousness is a necessary, but not a sufficient, condition of a creature's being a For-itself. Animals are certainly much more like Beings-in-themselves, despite their manifest consciousness.

In the nothingness which lies at the heart of human beings there is an endless number of possibilities. Since there is no Human Nature as such, there is no necessity for a man to determine himself in one direction rather than another. His possibilities include the possibility of answering 'No' to every suggestion, not only of what he should do, but also of what he should think, or even how he should describe and categorize what he perceives in the world. When a man really sees for the first time that this nothingness exists within himself (in other words, that he is free to do and to think whatever he chooses), he suffers Anguish. He is unable to bear the thought of his boundless freedom, and in order to escape from this anguish, he often adopts the cover of Bad Faith. This takes the form of pretending to himself that he is not as free as he actually is. Bad faith is the Sartrean equivalent of inauthenticity.

At this stage, it is very hard to interpret Sartre exactly. For nowhere else does his characteristic exaggeration create as many difficulties as in the general discussion of freedom. If it is really true that we each of us frame our own categories, determine our own ways of looking at the world, and our own ways of feeling about it, then, since we most of us never *feel* in the least bit free in any of these matters, we must all of us be far gone in self-deception and Bad Faith. It does not seem as if we had any choice at all, for example, in the practice of distinguishing blue from yellow as a colour. It is irrelevant to argue that there have been peoples who have had no words in their language by which they could draw any such distinction. No one perhaps would wish to say that the categories of blue and yellow are absolutely *essential* to any description of the world. It is only that, belonging as we do to a race which has the two words 'blue' and 'yellow' at its disposal, and supposing that we are neither blind nor colour-blind, and that we have been brought up in a normal way among users of the two words, then it does look very much as though to use them in the ordinary way is not really a matter of choice at all. Obviously anyone could choose to misuse the two words, and either substitute one for the other, or use them at random. But what such a person would be doing would be choosing to refuse to communicate in the language which his compatriots use. He would not be choosing to adopt *a new method of description*. If the feeling that we are bound to describe something as blue when it is seen and agreed to be blue, as yellow when it is seen and agreed to be yellow—if this feeling is Bad Faith, then certainly we are all guilty of Bad Faith every time we open our mouths. Choosing the right word is not choosing according to our personal fancy, but choosing what will be the best and most informative word *used in its agreed or conventional sense*. At least, this is the normal case. There is a vast difference between saying, on the one hand, that human beings in general invent their own ways of categorizing the world around them, and that there is no single inevitable way that they should do this, and saying on the other hand that *each* human being chooses his *own* categories. The former is probably true, the latter certainly false.

But let us concede that Sartre was here guilty either of confusion or at least of gross exaggeration, and let us nevertheless give due attention to the concept of Bad Faith, as that device which protects us from the anguish of recognizing that we are freer than we like to think. We may take it that nobody suffers the anguished recognition of his own freedom all the time, or even very often. For the most part we feel as much committed to our way of life, to our tastes and values, as we do to the very language that we speak. Values, Sartre says 'spring up around us like partridges' when we take a step in any direction. But every now and then, perhaps because of some war or revolution, perhaps because of some personal crisis, people are forced to think about their values, and it will be then that they face their freedom in anguish. They will find themselves bereft of all the ordinary ways of thought, of all the comforting beliefs that one *must* work, that one *must* be loyal, that one *must* support one's family or regard human life as sacred. When they realize that they may value anything as they please, and moreover that they have no character to guide their choice except that which they chose for themselves, that they are not *essentially* members of a certain profession or class, then they experience anguish at their emptiness, their vacancy, and at that private non-existence which is identical with their freedom.

Thus for Sartre's man, nothingness does not appal because it is the end of everything, nor because, in thinking about things, he sees them swirling about between Being and Not-being. Nothingness appals him because it is *part of himself*, and both he cannot escape from it, and it prevents him from completely absorbing himself in any other project. I am nothing. I cannot completely become anything, in the solid inevitable way that a tree is a tree, or an inkwell an inkwell. Because of the nature of consciousness itself (or, as I have suggested, of language-using), whatever a man does, he is always capable of contrasting what he is doing both with what other people and things are doing, and with what he might be doing, but is not, and with what he would be doing if he were a Being-in-itself, wholly describable by a description of his acts. Bad Faith would not be possible except to a creature who was capable both of self-consciousness, in the minimal pre-reflective manner, and of negation; for it consists in seeing what one is, and denying it; asserting that one *is* what one *is* not.

Besides these two capacities, it is, according to Sartre, a simple fact about human beings that they are able to hold two contradictory beliefs at one and the same time, or to believe and not believe the same thing at the same time (and in saying that people can do this he is manifestly right). So, even though in the kind of argument we are here considering, Sartre is ostensibly moving from those very general features of the world, contained in the distinction between Beings-in-themselves and Beings-for-themselves, he has recourse even here to quite ordinary psychological observations of how human beings behave; and these observations form part of his premise. His metaphysical intuition is constantly supported by his novelist's eye for human idiosyncrasy. The conclusion of the argument from the general to the particular is that human beings are capable of very specific kinds of self-deception, and that their general relationship with the world makes it inevitable that they should practise it.

In Bad Faith there is no cynical lie nor knowing preparation for deceitful concepts. The first act of Bad Faith, on the other hand, is to flee what it cannot flee, to flee what it is. The very project of flight reveals to Bad Faith an inner disintegration in the heart of being, and it is this disintegration which Bad Faith wishes to be. In truth, the two

immediate attitudes which we can take in the face of our being are con-
ditioned by the nature of this being and its relation with the in-itself.
Good Faith seeks to flee the inner disintegration of my being in the
direction of the in-itself which it should be and is not. Bad Faith seeks
to flee the in-itself by means of the inner disintegration of my being.
But it denies this disintegration, as it denies that it is itself Bad Faith. . . .
If Bad Faith is possible, it is because it is an immediate permanent threat
to every project of the human being; it is because consciousness conceals
in its being a permanent risk of Bad Faith. The origin of this risk is
the fact that the nature of consciousness is simultaneously to be what
it is not, and not to be what it is.[1]

Bad Faith is, he elsewhere says, 'a certain art of forming contradictory concepts which unite in themselves both an idea and the
negation of that idea'. Having thus derived Bad Faith from the
ultimate structure of human reality, Sartre can then go on to
illustrate it by means of some of his most memorable exemplary
anecdotes.

Coming back for a moment to our earlier objection, it will be
noticed that Sartre says that Bad Faith is a *risk* built in to the
nature of consciousness. He does not say that we are all necessarily
in Bad Faith all the time. On the other hand, he also suggests in
the passage quoted above that Good Faith, or honesty, is usually
itself only another form of Bad Faith, a different method of escap-
ing the anguish of freedom, by avowing one's faults, and thus
seeming to render one's viciousness a kind of inevitable characteristic which one has, in the way that objects in the world have
inevitable characteristics. Sartre writes of the 'honest' man

who cannot see that the honest man constitutes himself as a thing in
order to escape the condition of a thing by the same act of honesty. The
man who confesses that he is evil has exchanged his disturbing 'freedom
of will' for an inanimate character of evil; he is evil, he clings to himself, he is what he is. But by the same act of confession, he escapes from
the *thing* since it is he who contemplates it, since it depends on him to
maintain it or let it collapse into an infinity of separate acts. He derives
merit from his honesty, and the meritorious man is not the evil man in
so far as he is evil, but only in so far as he has passed beyond his evilness.[2]

So Bad Faith and so-called Good Faith or honesty are really two

---

[1] *Being and Nothingness*, pt. i, ch. 2, sec. 3. The translations from this work
are by Mrs. Christine North. Except for this passage and the next, they were
first published in Mary Warnock: *The Philosophy of Sartre* (Hutchinson,
London, 1965).

[2] op. cit., pt. i, ch. 2, sec. 2.

different forms of the same flight from reality, which is possible and likely because of the incomplete, empty and 'nothing-like' nature of human beings, a nature which goes inevitably with their intelligence and ability to describe and discourse about the world. If there is an authenticity, a way of avoiding this great pitfall, Sartre does not disclose it; indeed in a footnote to *Being and Nothingness* he says that the description of authenticity has no place in his present work. So much for the arguments from the general nature of man.

If we look next at the arguments which move from the particular to the general, we shall find that the position is rather better. Provided that Bad Faith is a *possibility* for human beings, then Sartre can draw his conclusion that Nothingness is an esential part of consciousness, since Bad Faith would not be possible without it. He therefore proceeds to describe two different kinds of Bad Faith. In the first kind a human being tries to believe, while knowing at the same time that it is pretence, that he is just a thing, and therefore cannot help behaving as he is behaving. It is obvious that this mode of Bad Faith is very close indeed to what Sartre describes as the Good Faith of the honest man, who confesses that he *just is* weak, wicked, a homosexual, or whatever it is, and thus absolves himself from the responsibility, either of being like this, or of trying to be otherwise. It is also clear that, when one pretends to be a thing rather than a free conscious being, one is likely to invoke the concept of causation. One's actions will, according to such an account, be determined by purely physical causes as are the actions of a ball which is being bounced, or a bit of paper which is being blown in the wind.

Sartre illustrates this mode of Bad Faith by his story (which incidentally has also been used by Simone de Beauvoir) of a girl who is taken to a restaurant by a man, and who, in order to preserve the excitement of the occasion, and to put off the moment when she must face making a definite decision, saying either 'yes' or 'no' to him, pretends to herself that she does not notice his intentions towards her. There finally comes a moment when he takes her hand; and the moment of decision would be upon her, only at this very moment she becomes totally absorbed in intellect-ual conversation, and leaves her hand to be taken by him, without noticing it, as if he has just picked up some *thing*, any thing, off the table. She has dissociated herself from her hand, for the time being, and is pretending to herself that it is nothing whatever to do with her. Her hand just rests in his hand, inert and thing-like. If she had removed it, or deliberately left it where it was, she would in either case have manifestly come to some decision. But by simply not taking responsibility for her hand and what happened to it, she avoided the need to decide; and this is Bad Faith. Here is an anecdote which really works, in the sense that the girl is instantly recognizable, and indeed we may go further, and not merely say 'there is a type I know' but 'there am I'. So Bad Faith is possible, because, as we now agree, it occurs. And therefore it *must* be possible for human consciousness to reflect upon its situation in this peculiar asserting–denying manner, which in turn derives from its free power to negate, or to assert what is not the case.

The second kind of Bad Faith is introduced by Sartre's portrait of an over-acting waiter. (Once again, such a figure appears in Simone de Beauvoir as well, as a barman.) All the movements and gestures of the waiter are slightly over-done. His behaviour is essentially ritualistic. He bends forward in a manner which is too deeply expressive of concern and deference for the diners; he balances his tray in a manner which is just a little too precarious. His movements are all of them like the movements in a mime or a game. The game which he is playing is the game of 'being a waiter'. He is quite consciously acting out the role of waiter, and executing the peculiar waiter's 'dance'. 'The waiter in the café plays with his condition in order to realize it.' He wishes, that is to say, to make his condition real, so that he shall have no choices left, but shall be completely and wholly absorbed in being a waiter. Not only does he want this himself, but there is pressure upon him from outside to do this. For the general public wishes to be able to think of him simply and solely as a waiter. They do not want to have to think of him as a free human agent, but prefer that he should be nothing but the character demanded by his job.

Of all tradesmen, Sartre says: 'The public demands of them that they realize their condition as a ceremony; there is the dance of the grocer, of the tailor, of the auctioneer, by which they endeavour to persuade their clientele that they are nothing but a grocer, an auctioneer, a tailor. A grocer who dreams is offensive to the customer because he is not wholly a grocer. . . . There are indeed many precautions for imprisoning a man in what he is, as if we lived in perpetual fear that he might escape from it, that he might break away, and suddenly elude his condition.'

On the other hand, from within, the waiter knows that he *cannot* be wholly and completely a waiter and nothing else at all, as an inkwell is an inkwell; since the mere fact that he can reflect on his condition precludes such a solid and total existence within the situation. The abstract idea of a waiter, with all the rights and duties which go with the idea, is something which no human being can completely fulfil. The 'ideal' waiter is a representation, not something actual; and so one can only *represent* the waiter as oneself. 'But if I represent myself as him, I am not he; I am separate from him as the object from the subject, separated by *nothing*—but this nothing isolates me from him; that is, I imagine to myself that I am he.'

What the waiter, in acting out his part, is attempting to make real is the Being-in-itself of the café waiter. He is pretending that, given that he is a waiter (that is to say, given that he actually earns his money this way, and he is not a farmer or an ambassador), it is absolutely inevitable that he should behave in certain ways. He is pretending that it was not he who had in fact imposed this necessity upon himself. Bad Faith consists in pretending to oneself that one is bound by necessity, and has no choices open to one. This *is* pretence; for obviously the waiter *could* choose not to get up in the morning, not to make the coffee, not to be polite to the customers and so on. If he did not fulfil his duty, he would doubtless be sacked. But he could perfectly well choose to be sacked. However far one presses it, the waiter could value things differently. It is no good his saying that he must work to support his wife and family. Why must he support them? He could choose to let them starve. It is precisely the realization that to value things as he does and to accept the consequences of this evaluation is his own decision, which causes that Anguish which Bad Faith is intended to make bearable. The waiter is a waiter 'in the mode of Being-what-he-is-not'.

This is the conclusion which Sartre draws from his verbal portrait. He is therefore able to deduce that such behaviour would be impossible without the human ability to conceive of that which is not, and to transcend, conceptually, any particular situation. This transcendence is identical with the separation from one's

situation which, as we have already seen, is the essential characteristic of consciousness. Thus the existence of Bad Faith, established by means of acceptable and recognizable descriptions of
kinds of human behaviour which are familiar to us, is taken to
prove that consciousness is as Sartre says it is, compounded of
distance or nothingness, which is what sets conscious nature apart
from non-conscious nature.

It is perhaps worth noticing that the people who emerge in the
anecdotes in *Being and Nothingness* are like people as imagined
by Kierkegaard. It was Kierkegaard who conceived of the anguish
of Abraham. When Abraham heard the voice commanding him to
sacrifice his son, he took it to be a command from heaven, and he
obeyed it. But afterwards he might have realized that it was *he* who
interpreted the command as divine. There could never be any
conclusive proof that it was so. The responsibility, therefore, for
the sacrifice of Isaac could not have been shuffled off onto God.
It was Abraham, and he alone, who decided to obey the voice. He
alone was entirely responsible for his acts. Similarly, for Sartrean
man it is of no use to try to evade the responsibility entailed
in total freedom. Beings-for-themselves are simply constituted
free, and cannot get out of it. But Bad Faith is one of their methods
of trying to do so.

It is not entirely clear whether Sartre thinks that people are
to be blamed for falling into Bad Faith or not. Although, as we
have seen, in a footnote, he contrasts both Bad and Good Faith with
Authenticity, he has nothing to say about the latter; and perhaps
he would agree with Heidegger in disclaiming any evaluative sense
in his use of the term 'Authentic' (which he uses, in fact, very
seldom). But the most extended and elaborate treatment of Bad
Faith is contained in the book on Genet, and here there is a kind
of pity for Genet who was driven, like the waiter, to playing out
the role, this time as thief and criminal, which society had assigned
to him. But, in the end, for him, the way of salvation was found,
in literature. Genet came to realize for himself that he had *chosen*
to live as a criminal, because once upon a time he had stolen from
his foster-parents and had been labelled a thief. Realizing that it
was a matter of decision, he was able to reverse the decision, and
self-consciously work out his salvation in writing. His initial Bad
Faith was the result of 'transcending' his situation, and determining to represent himself as that which society expected him to be.

His escape was equally a consequence of standing back from his life and, having set it at a distance from himself, seeing it for the play-acting that it was.

The basic fact, then, which is proved by the characteristic human behaviour of Bad Faith is that in a world of things, there exists also, unaccountably, consciousness, which is aware of the things around it, and also of itself; which is separate from the world, and therefore able to conceive both how the world is and how it is not. This distance from the world produces not only human freedom but also the power of imagination, which essentially consists in representing things as they might be, but are not.

Sartre also speaks of the Nothingness which constitutes consciousness as a 'lack'. The existence of desire as a human fact, he says, is sufficient to prove that human reality is a lack. What human beings lack is, of course, the completeness of existence which belongs to Beings-in-themselves which are through and through whatever it is that they are; which have essences, and which are solid. Sartre thinks that the attribute of solidity, of being *massif*, is intrinsically preferable to the attribute of hollowness. All creatures, he believes, have, as their deepest instinct, the instinct to fill up holes, and to abolish emptiness wherever they find it. So human beings long to possess the solidity of things. But if they were solid and complete, they would necessarily lose their consciousness. And they do not wish to become unconscious. Thus, what they wish for is a contradiction; they wish to be conscious, and at the same time *massif*.

This impossible goal towards which the Being-for-itself strives is the supreme value (sometimes called God). It is just because the goal is contradictory, and therefore necessarily unattainable, that the free human consciousness can always move towards it, beyond whatever is its present state. This value arises immediately, like freedom itself, out of the vacancy within the human being. Sartre says that value, in its original upsurge, is not posited by the For-itself; on the contrary, it is 'consubstantial' with it. There is no consciousness which is not haunted by its own value. 'It is present and out of reach, and it is simply lived as the concrete meaning of that lack which makes my present being.'

It will be seen that, on Sartre's thesis about the nature of consciousness, it is impossible to describe the relation between conscious beings and the world as purely perceptual or cognitive.

Immediately, into the logical foundation of the connection between Beings-for-themselves and Beings-in-themselves there enters an element of emotion: a yearning on the part of consciousness to become something which it cannot become. (It will be recollected that for Heidegger, too, the basic connection between people and their world was that of 'Sorge' or Concern.) A conscious being's attitude to the world in which he exists is never one of dispassionate enquiry; or not of this alone. A man longs to become in some sense thinglike, and so he envies, loves, hates, desires things, as well as either just observing or just using them. Sartre would deny that perception of the world *can* be isolated and examined as a phenomenon on its own. Merleau-Ponty aimed to show that perception cannot be 'bare' perception, as envisaged by Hume or the Phenomenalists. He argued that perception of objects is always a matter of perceiving significance or meaning in our world. We are 'condemned to meaning'. Sartre would go further and would not wish to draw any distinction between perceiving and experiencing emotion.

In his early *Sketch for a Theory of the Emotions,* he argued for a definition of emotion as intentional, that is, as directed towards an object. Emotion is in fact, he suggested, a particular kind of perception; it is a certain way of apprehending the world. Instead of seeing the world as governed by causal laws, to experience emotion is to see it as governed by magic. When I am gripped by fear at the sight of a face at the window, it is because I see the face as belonging to someone who could get at me and destroy me immediately, even though in fact I may be safely locked into my house. When I stamp my foot in rage, it is because I cannot really, in the real world, trample my enemy under foot, but I believe for the time in the magical world in which he will be destroyed by my stamping. Whenever the apprehension of an object gives rise to unbearable tension, the consciousness tries to apprehend it otherwise, or does so without trying. The emotion may take the form of our seeing the object in a new light, for instance when, in disappointment at not being able to reach some grapes, we see them as green and unripe; or it may take the form of our transforming ourselves, the observers. We may relieve the tension by fainting, or by weeping, so that we cannot perceive the offending object any more. All this is to suggest that perception, feeling, and action are logically connected. Emotion is a way of perceiving; it is also an incipient action. We operate upon the world, we feel moved by the world, we perceive the world. All these happen together. We see the world from a certain point of view, with certain purposes, and in a certain light, not just sometimes, but always.

That was Sartre's early doctrine. His view of the connection between emotion and perception had not changed by the time he came to write *Being and Nothingness*. There are three main emotions or attitudes which he believed we must necessarily adopt in face of the world, given that consciousness and the world are as they are. The first of these emotions is anguish, about which enough has already been said. The second response which we are bound to have is the feeling of *absurdity*, or of the dispensableness of everything. The third response is a feeling of *nausea* in the face of certain characteristics of Beings-in-themselves.

The first two of these emotions derive wholly or entirely from the conscious being's perception of himself. He experiences anguish, as we have seen, upon the contemplation of his own freedom. The sense of the absurd arises in a somewhat similar way. Nothing is absurd or *de trop* if it is an integral part of a rational plan. So, as long as we skate across the surface of our life, taking our plans and projects seriously, believing that there are things we *have* to do and materials or tools which we *have* to use to do them, we will not suffer from the sense of the absurd. But as soon as we contemplate our own *facticity*, then all this is changed.

The facticity of a human being is the particular set of contingent facts that are true of him and of him alone. For each one of us there is such a set of facts, concerned with our parents, our date of birth, the physical appearance which we happen to possess, and so on. We tend to take these facts for granted, as a necessary part of each one of us; but though it is true that everyone must have some parents, some sort of appearance, hair of some colour or other, there is no possible *reason* why one of these features in particular should be present rather than another, for any particular person. There is no possible *point* in our being as we are. 'I cannot doubt', Sartre says, 'that I am. But in so far as *this* For-itself, as such, could also not be, that I exist has all the contingency of fact. Just as my nihilating freedom is apprehended in anguish, so the For-itself is conscious of its facticity. It has the feeling of its complete gratuitousness; it apprehends itself as being there for nothing, as being *de trop*.'

It is hardly necessary to elaborate upon the kinds of devices of Bad Faith by which we can mitigate for ourselves this disagreeable feeling. Obviously if one can believe that one's life *has* a purpose, that one has some missionary or other task to fulfil which could be fulfilled by no one else, then the sense of the absurdity of one's existence will vanish. Similarly the ordinary objects of everyday life will no longer seem pointless or dispensable, if one can think of them as necessary means for some genuinely important or necessary end. The absurd is closely related to the futile, and the sense of futility is not felt by those who are sufficiently self-important.

The third response to the world which Sartre believes that conscious beings must experience is disgust or nausea. All our contact with the world, whether in perception, emotion or action, is contact through the medium of our own awareness of our bodies. The body is as crucial a part of our general consciousness on Sartre's as on Merleau-Ponty's theory. But the actual quality of this awareness of the body, without which a man cannot be aware of anything else, is, according to Sartre, the quality of nausea. Nausea is thus a kind of physiological counterpart of 'prereflective consciousness'. I carry it around with me inevitably as long as I am alive. Very often I do not notice this nausea, because I am fully engaged in some other feeling or activity; but when the particular activity ceases, the nausea is found, after all, to have persisted. Sartre writes:

In particular we must note that when no pain, no particular satisfaction or dissatisfaction is experienced by consciousness, the For-itself does not therefore cease to project itself beyond a pure and unqualified contingency. Consciousness, that is, does not cease to 'have' a body. . . . This perpetual apprehension on the part of the For-itself of an insipid taste, which I cannot place, which accompanies me even in my efforts to get away from it, this we have described under the name of nausea. A dull and inescapable nausea perpetually reveals my body to my consciousness. Sometimes we look for the pleasant or for physical pain to free ourselves from this nausea; but as soon as the pain or the pleasure are experienced by consciousness they manifest its facticity and its contingency, and it is against the background of nausea that they are revealed.[1]

[1] op. cit., pt. iii, ch. 2, sec. 1.

It is not only in the apprehension of our bodies that we experience nausea. We are also filled with the same nausea on becoming
aware of certain key-aspects of the world. The very nature of
existence itself disgusts us. Sometimes Sartre seems to envisage a
man's being overcome by disgust, as Roquentin was in the novel
La Nausée, at the thought of the frightful teeming unmanageable
mass of material of which the world is made. Part of the terror
felt by the conscious being in the face of the world is the terror
that he cannot properly manage his environment. He wishes to
label and tabulate things but they are not amenable to such
discipline. Roquentin, looking at the roots of a chestnut tree in
the park, suddenly saw it as *existing*, untouched by all the descriptions he might give of it, part of an undifferentiated mass of *being*;
and all the ways in which he normally thought about things seemed
at that moment to be superficial and silly. Roquentin reflects that
in the past he took things in his hand, he used them as tools, he
described them.

But all that was happening on the surface. If anyone had asked what
existence was, I should have replied in all good faith that it wasn't
anything, just an empty form which was added to external things, without in any way changing their nature. But suddenly there it was, as
clear as day; existence was revealed. It had lost its inoffensive look of an
abstract category; it was the very stuff of things . . . The roots, the park
railings, the bench, the sparse grass on the lawn, had all disappeared;
the diversity, the individuality of things was a mere illusion, a veneer.
The veneer had splintered, leaving monstrous flabby, disorganized
masses—naked; terrifyingly and obscenely naked.[1]

This is a new kind of answer to Heidegger's enquiry about existence itself—what it is *like* to exist. It is disgusting.

If this is, according to Sartre, the aspect of nature which can
at any time be revealed to us, obviously those natural objects which,
without any special revelation, possess this kind of features, the
spreading sticky amorphous features which Roquentin saw in the
tree stump, will exercise a peculiar fascination for us, as revealing
the true nature of reality; and they will disgust us accordingly.

Sartre believes that an Existentialist ought to be able to provide
a 'psycho-analysis of things', which would be an explanation of
why it was that people liked or disliked, feared or welcomed,
different textures, tastes, appearances in the physical world. To

[1] *Nausea*, trans. L. Alexander (Hamish Hamilton, London, 1962), p. 171.

do this would be to reveal the *meaning* that each kind of quality had for each person. This is, of course, an idea familiar from Freud. But there are some general meanings, Sartre thought, against the background of which particular idiosyncratic systems of meaningfulness would be displayed.

One item in the general list would be the disgust and fear felt by a conscious being when he contemplates the viscosity or stickiness of things. For any conscious being this quality of viscosity stands for all that is beyond his power to manage in the world of existent things. There is a sense in which the fact that things exist in the world at all is a kind of threat to consciousness; and viscous things bring clearly to light what this threat is. To touch the viscous is to risk being dissolved in viscosity. Now this dissolution by itself is frightening enough, because it is the absorption of the For-itself in the In-itself, as ink is absorbed by the blotter. But it is still more frightening in that the metamorphosis is not just into a thing, but into the *viscous*.

A consciousness which became viscous would be transformed by the thick stickiness of its ideas. From the time of our upsurge into the world we are haunted by the image of a consciousness which would like to launch forth into the future, and which at the very moment when it was conscious of arriving at its own projection, would be held back slyly by the invisible suction of the past, and would have to assist in its own slow dissolution in this past which it was fleeing. The horror of the viscous is the horrible fear that time might become viscous, that facticity and contingency might insensibly absorb the For-itself. It is the fear, not of death, not of the pure In-itself, not of nothingness, but of a particular type of being which does not actually exist any more than any other ideal, and which is only represented by the viscous. It is an ideal being which I reject with all my strength and which haunts me as value haunts my being, an ideal being in which the In-itself has priority over the For-itself. We shall call it an Anti-value.[1]

Here, then, we have the crucial element in the connection between consciousness and the world. It is a kind of horrified fear of inert and lifeless matter which we may see, in a nightmare, as taking over and destroying the elaborate values and purposes in life which we have constructed for ourselves. We may conceive it as sucking us into a whirling and sweetly sticky, sickening morass. It is in a world where the conscious Being-for-himself has to create

[1] *Being and Nothingness*, pt. iv, ch. 2, sec. 3.

his life amid such hideous fantasies, that Sartre is supposed to be able to say what kind of a life this should be. In the next chapter I shall discuss first the relation which Sartre believes to hold, not now between people and the world, but between one person and another (Being for-others). I shall go on to discuss the nature of Sartre's philosophy, in so far as it is practical. Enough has been said, perhaps, to show that there is no very hard and fast line to be drawn in Existentialism between practical or ethical philosophy and theories about the nature of the universe. If this line cannot be drawn for Existentialists in general, least of all can it be drawn for Sartre.

6
Jean-Paul Sartre (2)

SARTRE has very often been thought of primarily as a writer on moral philosophy. It is my business in this chapter to see what his moral philosophy actually consisted in, and to describe as far as possible the manner in which, in pursuing his undoubted interest in making people different, in getting them to see themselves and to behave in certain ways, he ceased in the end to be an Existentialist. The later writings of Sartre fall outside the scope of this book altogether.

The elements of moral philosophy must be looked for in the context of theories of social or inter-personal relations, and it is for this reason that it is necessary first to discover what Sartre had to say, in *Being and Nothingness,* about our existence in the mode of Being-for-others.

We have seen that consciousness knowingly places itself at a distance from its objects, and that the gap between itself and its objects is identical both with the power to confirm or deny what it chooses, and also with the power to act upon the world in order to try to realize a future which it can foresee. Freedom and consciousness are the very same thing. Only the free consciousness can imagine a world different from that in which it finds itself, and therefore it alone can form plans to change that world. However, despite the apparently endless freedom built into the nature of conscious things, they are in fact constrained in various directions. For one thing, each person has, as we have seen, his own 'facticity' which limits the possibilities open to him. We shall return to this shortly. There is also a further factor limiting freedom. Just as people are supposed by Sartre inevitably to adopt certain emotional attitudes towards the world of things, so they are, to some extent, equally predictable in their relations with others.

In discussing Being-for-others Sartre first argues against solipsism and seeks to show how we *know*, without doubt, that other people exist. This part of *Being and Nothingness* is in many ways the best in the book, and Sartre is particularly clear and illuminating as a critic of Heidegger's view of *Mitsein*. But his own method of proof of the existence of others is highly typical of his version of Existentialism, and is therefore worth considering in its own right. His argument is that we can recognize the mode of Being-for-others as a radically different mode of being from any other; and that therefore there cannot be any question but that other people exist. We experience their existence in our bones. To show that we do have such an experience of recognition of this mode of being, he describes a concrete situation which we can feel to be plausible.

He describes a man who, moved by jealousy or curiosity, looks through a keyhole and listens at a door. He is, for the time being, completely absorbed in what he is doing, in such a way that his consciousness of himself and his body is reduced to the minimum of prereflective consciousness. He has no attention left over from what he is doing to describe himself or to *say* what he is doing. He sees the door, the keyhole, and all his surroundings as part of the task he has set himself, given to him as means or as obstacles in his path. But now, suddenly, he hears a foostep in the hall behind him. He realizes that someone is there watching him. He is transformed. His existence is reconstituted in a wholly new way. He suddenly exists, not just as a series of aims and actions, but as a *person eavesdropping*. He realizes that he would be described by the other man as 'caught in the act', 'bent down to peer through the keyhole' and so on; and these descriptions do not seem alien from him. He accepts them as belonging properly to him. He suddenly springs into existence as an object which can be looked at from outside, as an object capable of bearing descriptive labels, a *thing* such as can be truly or falsely described. He accepts these descriptions of himself in *shame*.

This anecdote, which is told in Sartre's most direct and memorable manner, is simply intended to make us recollect the emotion of shame, as it is actually experienced. The point of the story is, of course, to bring out the difference which comes about in the man at the very moment at which it is appropriate for him to feel shame, and he feels it. He is altered, Sartre says, in the structure of his being. When we are made to imagine the moment of shock at which he realizes that he is under observation, we are also supposed to be made to understand a profound philosophical truth, namely that we exist, essentially, *in relation to other people*. Other people are not, as Descartes tried to make us believe, merely coats and hats for us, beneath which we have to *infer* the existence of beings rather like ourselves. People exist in a full-blooded way, and we know that they do directly, and without inference of any kind, because we know that we ourselves would exist differently if they did not. This knowledge is part of our knowledge of ourselves. Our life cannot be lived entirely at the level of pre-reflective self-consciousness. We are sometimes like the man at the keyhole, made aware of ourselves in a different way, in shame, which reveals that we are exposed to the comments of others. This, then, constitutes Sartre's proof that other people exist.

From this same story another important factor in our relations with others emerges. The man at the keyhole, when he was discovered, immediately began to apply labels or descriptions to himself, and his shame arose from the knowledge that these same descriptions would rightly be applied by the person who was watching him. He was aware of himself, that is, as an object for other people. That other people describe us in certain ways has, as we have seen, an important effect on our behaviour. We may choose to live in Bad Faith, denying our true freedom, in order to live out the roles which have been allotted us by other people. Thus Genet devoted himself to his life of crime, and Sartre's waiter overplayed his waiter's role. According to Heidegger, to be absorbed in the judgements and evaluation of others is what leads to inauthentic existence, and to our discourse being mere prattling. But Sartre pursues a further consequence of this tendency which people have to type-cast their fellow men.

Heidegger sees human beings as seeking in some sense to disengage themselves from society, in order to pursue authentic existence. Sartre goes further, and also describes from the other end the desire which we have to capture other people, and to make them conform to our type-casting. One of the horrifying features of reality, as it revealed itself to Roquentin in the park in *La Nausée*, was that being, actual concrete existence, could not be wholly contained in the ordinary categories of language. It flowed out at the edges of our categories in a messy and threatening way. Human beings are naturally prone to want material objects to be completely predictable and completely under their control. The horror and nausea engendered by the viscous is in fact caused, not only by the tactile quality itself, but still more by the threat contained in such substances as pitch or treacle, that they may flow everywhere and overwhelm one; that if one is caught by them, one will never be able to escape, but will be sucked down like the wasp in the jam-jar. The opposite of this treacle-like creeping stuff is neatly labelled *types* of things, each governed by an established set of laws, each separated by a tidy definition from every other type.

Now, if there exists such a human longing for orderly control in the universe, one would expect it to manifest itself in our relations with other human beings as well as in our relations with Beings-in-themselves. And so Sartre thinks that it does. We wish people to conform to the descriptions we give of them. We wish to predict their behaviour entirely, according to the role in which we have cast them. Our reason for wishing this, in the case of other people, is even stronger than it is in the case of inanimate objects. For other people are essentially, in themselves, and by their very existence, a danger to us. Once I realize that I am an object of observation to the Other, I also realize that he will have his own ways of assessing and of trying to predict my behaviour. I will reciprocate, and likewise try to reduce him to the status of a thing. But I know, all the time, that I cannot entirely succeed in doing this. When I see another human being, a man, reading his book, let us say, in a public garden, I experience him partly as a mere physical object; but I am aware that to describe him in purely physical terms is inadequate. The fact that he is *reading* constitutes an all-important difference between him and any other object. He is thinking his own thoughts, understanding the words through the medium of his own perceptions, and orientating round himself a whole new world, which is *his* world, not mine. He escapes me, in some essential part of himself. Sartre speaks of the relation between the reading man and his book as a little crack in my universe. 'It appears', he says, 'as if the world has a kind of drain hole in the middle of its being, and that it is perpetually flowing off through this hole.' The man is an object for me, but of a peculiarly slippery and evasive kind.

Thus, both because the Other will observe me and try to make me an object for himself by describing me, and because he escapes me, ultimately, in my attempts to describe him or pin him down, the presence of other people in the world constitutes a 'scandal'. It is a constant source of threat and alarm. Sartre, incidentally, uses this very fact as a further conclusive argument against solipsism. My awareness of other people cannot be a mere inference.

The fact of the Other is incontestable, and touches me to the heart. I realize him through uneasiness; through him I feel myself perpetually in danger. The Other does not appear to me as a being who is constituted first, so as to encounter me later; he appears as a being who arises in an original relation of being with me, and whose indubitable necessity and factual necessity are those of my own consciousness.[1]

The fact that the man who caught his fellow man at the keyhole will label him 'an eavesdropper' can thus be seen to contain within it the essence of the whole relationship between one human being and another—the essence of conflict. The freedom of another person is the most fatal obstacle to my own freedom to do as I wish. The existence of more than one free agent in the world (that is, of more than one conscious being) of necessity engenders conflict. The look of the Other is, Sartre says, the death of my possibilities.

To remain at home because it is raining, and to remain at home because one has been forbidden to go out are by no means the same thing. It is not mere caprice which causes us often to do, without annoyance, what would have irritated us if another had commanded it. It is because the order and the prohibition cause us to experience the other's freedom as our own slavery.[2]

The details of the conflict between one human being and another are contained in the third chapter of Part III of *Being and Nothingness*. Sartre says,

While I attempt to free myself from the hold of the Other, the Other is trying to free himself from mine; while I seek to enslave the Other, the Other seeks to enslave me . . . Descriptions of concrete behaviour must be seen within the perspective of *conflict*.[3]

In particular, this conflict is fierce and hopeless where the concrete behaviour in question is the behaviour of love. Love is not

[1] *Being and Nothingness*, pt. iii, ch. 1, sec. 4.
[2] loc. cit.   [3] loc. cit.

primarily to be explained in terms of 'ownership'. Sartre argues that if it were, lovers might often be satisfied. But the reason why the lover wishes to possess his loved one is that he is, in a sense, *created* by the other, by the free voluntary choice of the other. It is the other's consciousness—that is, his freedom—which the lover wants to possess, that consciousness which among other things is consciousness *of* him, which sees him and treats him as an object in the world. But of course what the lover wants is a contradiction, and so he can never be satisfied, for if he possessed this freedom, then his loved one would no longer *be* free. Freedom cannot be possessed.

> The man who wants to be loved does not really desire the enslavement of the beloved. He is not bent on becoming the object of a devotion which flows forth automatically . . . The total enslavement of the beloved kills the love of the lover. If the beloved is transformed into an automaton the lover finds himself alone. Thus the lover demands a special type of appropriation. He wants to possess a freedom *as freedom*. But he demands that this freedom should be no longer free.[1]

Thus the lovers embark upon a hopeless struggle, each wanting wholly to limit the freedom of the other and yet to be loved by someone who is still free. A person cannot both be free and be a slave. Yet this is what the lovers demand. Within this hopeless and repetitive struggle, Sartre argues that there are only three possible patterns of behaviour. A lover may either become a sadist, and seek to appropriate the other completely and by violence. Or he may become a masochist, and consent to be nothing but a thing: simply an object for the consciousness of the other. Or he may adopt the attitude of indifference, which amounts to evading the conflict altogether.

These are the basic facts, on Sartre's theory, of our relations with other people. We must now see what he thinks human action is, and then go on to consider what possibilities there are for him to construct an ethical theory out of the materials thus presented in *Being and Nothingness*.

Action, as opposed to mere happening, entails a motive. A human action therefore arises from a thought about the world, a desire to change some feature in the agent's situation. It is only because we always perceive the world from the standpoint of

[1] loc. cit.

potential agents, and because we can project ourselves forward into a future which does not yet exist, that we can act at all. A mere state of affairs cannot be a motive in itself. Only the *awareness* of a state of affairs as something to be changed can motivate an action.

If a man is poor, or ill, he may regard his misfortune as an inevitable part of his life, and he may therefore live with his poverty or illness without ever thinking of a future without it. But, in so far as he is a conscious human being, a Being-for-himself, set at a distance from the world, he is nevertheless capable of imagining a life without poverty or illness. Once he has done this then he will have a motive to try to improve his situation. Although even when he thought his misfortune was inevitable he was in one way aware of it, he had it, at that time, as an object only for his non-reflective consciousness. As soon as he started to contemplate his situation, to detach himself from it and exercise upon it his faculty of description and of negation, then he could begin to plan deliberate action to mitigate or remove it.

Sartre insists, then, that it is the future, or rather the thought of the future, which causes us to act. We must consciously project ourselves into the future and away from the past if we are to act at all. Nothing will count as action which is not so motivated, and therefore it follows that no human action, properly so called, can arise out of or be caused by the past. He says:

> It is only by an absolute tearing away from himself and the world that a worker can regard his suffering as unbearable and therefore make of it the motive for revolutionary action. This implies for consciousness the permanent possibility of effecting a breach with its own past, so as to be able to consider it in the light of non-being and so as to be able to confer on it the meaning which it has in terms of the project of a meaning which it does not have. Under no circumstances can the past in any way by itself produce an act. In fact as soon as we attribute to consciousness this negative power with respect to the world and itself, as soon as the nihilation forms an integral part of positing an end, we must recognize that the indispensable fundamental condition of all action is the freedom of the agent.[1]

But it may well be argued that this kind of reference to the necessity of freedom in human action is a weak argument against determinism. Sartre has not really shown, it may be said, that human beings *are* free at all. He has argued only that *what he*

[1] op. cit., pt. iv, ch. 1, sec. 1.

means by action must be free. But perhaps no such thing as action, in his sense of the word, ever occurs. A convinced determinist would not in the least mind saying that action in this sense is a kind of myth, with no reality in the world. Against this, in turn, Sartre would simply say that we know that we are free because we can ourselves experience the *event* of choice, as it actually occurs. Since freedom is part of consciousness, we should not experience the world at all, unless we experienced it as free agents. We know that we must be free if we are conscious at all. The argument here may in some respects seem to be a repetition of the argument which we have already examined on the subject of Bad Faith. In that context, Sartre asked 'How is Bad Faith possible?' To this question, the answer was that it is possible if and only if the human consciousness contains Nothingness, and the possibility of Negation, within itself. Now we are asking 'How is action possible?' where 'action' means what we know that it does mean in our own experience. And the answer is exactly the same. Action is possible if and only if we can perceive the world at a distance, separated from ourselves by the gap in our consciousness which is Nothingness.

But the view that men are caused to act by their visions of the future rather than by any features of the past, although it does arise directly out of the theory of consciousness which is fundamental to *Being and Nothingness*, seems to take on an extra dimension in that it is also an anti-Freudian doctrine. Sartre wants, above all, to maintain the pure Existentialist dogma that we are what we choose to make ourselves, that we have no essences, no Human Nature, and no character that we did not confer upon ourselves. To believe that our characters are either given us from birth or formed inevitably by the events and circumstances of our early childhood is just as much to fall into Bad Faith as was Genet's acceptance of the role of thief assigned him by his foster parents. The function of Bad Faith, as we have seen, is to protect us from the recognition of our own responsibility. If we are honest, and are not corrupted or seduced by the comforting doctrines of Freud, we will recognize that nothing has formed our 'character', such as it is, except our own free choice.

It is through this belief in our own choice of character that Sartre partially solves the paradox of his apparently excessive claims to freedom. For we have seen that he allows each one of us to have his own facticity—the genuinely ineluctable circumstances

in which we are set down, and which plainly must be said by
common sense to limit our freedom. If I am only five foot tall, no
amount of wishing or will on my part will enable me to reach the
top shelves of a library without a step-ladder. So much Sartre of
course allows. But still my character is not formed by the mere
brute fact that I am very small. My diminutive height is simply
the raw material out of which I frame my free choices. The difference between me and another equally small person will be in the
different ways in which, as Sartre puts it, we 'live' our size. How we
experience our circumstances, how we live with them, how we
allow them to influence our outlook, our language, the kinds of
assumptions we make and the values we assign to things—all these
things are within our power to choose. For these, he claims, we are
wholly responsible.

So, though we none of us have any fixed or given complete
'character', and if we had we should be thing-like, solid *massif* in
the way that inanimate objects are, yet what is generally referred
to as our character is something which we have formed for ourselves out of the materials available to us. We cannot call upon
either our character or our past as an excuse for our behaving as
we do behave. Sartre has a long example by which he illustrates
this point in *Being and Nothingness*. He describes an expedition
into the country upon which a number of people of comparable
age and comparable physical fitness embark. One of them falls by
the way, flings down his rucksack and says that he is too tired to
go any further. Sartre analyses the decision that he is too tired. He
argues that for part of the walk this man will have experienced
his fatigue without really concentrating on it. He will have been
aware, but only in a minimal sense, that the path was steep, the
sun hot, his rucksack heavy, and his feet blistered. But at some
stage he will have detached himself from these phenomena, and
assigned a *value* to them.

He is like the workers who for a long time experience their
poverty as something inevitable, as merely the necessary condition
of life, but whose eyes are suddenly opened to the future, a possible
future with different elements; and at this stage they begin to
regard their poverty as unbearable, and as something which they
must take action against. In the same way the walker suddenly
evaluates his experiences, and describes them to himself as no
longer tolerable. And so, in this act of evaluation, he flings down

his pack and says that he cannot go on. 'As I become selfconscious, I regard what I am suffering as bearable or unbearable.' It is no use saying that one man gives up while the rest go on *because of the one man's character*. To say that the man who gives up is a 'feeble man' or 'weak' is to explain nothing. It is not to provide a causal explanation of his giving up; it is only to state the fact that he has given up, under another name. Neither is his giving up caused by the steepness of the slope or the heat of the sun. These are simply the factors in the situation which he chooses to regard in a particular light, as a challenge, as something to be enjoyed, or as something which he cannot bear. Sartre does not, he says, deny that the particular way that this man experiences his fatigue, and gives up the struggle, may be expressive of a general inferiority complex. But he would want to say that the inferiority complex itself is this particular man's way of projecting himself upon the world. 'It is my way of choosing myself.' And again,

It is impossible seriously to consider the feeling of inferiority without determining it with regard to the future and my possibilities. Even assertions such as 'I am ugly', 'I am stupid', are by nature anticipations. We are not dealing here with the pure establishing of my ugliness, but with the apprehension of the coefficient of adversity, which is presented . . . to my enterprises.[1]

Sartre goes on to argue that the brute facts of our life, the actual steepness of the hill, the heat of the sun, and so on, are necessary to freedom. Freedom cannot emerge except against a background of unchosen elements. But these elements do not *restrict* freedom; we are totally free in the manner in which we experience these elements. Our freedom to choose ourselves is limitless. An Existentialist psychoanalysis would seek to explain what it was that a man had chosen for himself in the future, rather than to explain the present in terms of the past.

It is worth remembering at this point that the acute hostility to Freudian theory, which Sartre manifests in this part of his work, is reflected in the horror of the viscous which, as we have seen, he regards as an absolutely inevitable feeling, encountered by any conscious being in his experience of the world. For part of the horror was a fear that time would itself become sticky and viscous and that, just as one was reaching forward into a chosen

[1] op. cit., pt. iv, ch. 1, sec. 2.

future, the sticky thick chaos of the past would suck one back into the condition of less-than-freedom. The idea that one is somehow a slave to the past is exceedingly horrible to Sartre, and the whole burden of his philosophy of freedom may be seen to be a rejection of the view that one is caused to act by things beyond one's control and even beyond one's memory. There is no honest excuse for one's behaviour or one's character to be derived from the plea that events of long ago made one as one is.

A man's character and his actions, then, arise out of the way in which, perceiving the world, he evaluates it; and his evaluations are entirely his own. No one can force me to value something high or low. Even if I take over my opinions from someone else, they become mine and I choose them. This, then, is the solution to the paradox of freedom. It is certainly true that I cannot choose entirely what I am or who my parents were or how strong I am. What I can choose is my *reaction to* my facticity. Sartre will countenance no further retreat into determinism.

But the fact, as he sees it, that our values are all of them chosen freely by us must have consequences for the possibility of constructing an ethical theory. Sartre is perfectly familiar with the truth, insisted upon by his contemporary English-speaking philosophers and others, that to evaluate something is not to describe it. It is, in fact, to choose it as a goal, to set it up as an ideal to be aimed at. There is therefore no question at all, in Sartre's view, of discovering any *absolute values* in the world. There just are no such things. If a man says that something is good or that it is bad, he is choosing it as a goal; he is not describing a property that it has. All moral philosophies tend, according to Sartre, to try to assert that something or other in the world has an absolute value, whether it is human happiness or some other thing. All moral philosophers are, in asserting such absolute values, succumbing to the 'Spirit of Seriousness' which is, of course, another form of Bad Faith. To suppose that values are somehow given is just to fall into the kind of refusal to face his freedom which afflicts the bourgeois respectable man, whose duties all seem to be laid out for him, and who believes that he is completely bound by the rules which govern his life. And yet Sartre could not possibly deny that we must evaluate things somehow or other. Nor would he want to deny this, since evaluation is built into action. Value is, he says, 'simply lived' at the very heart of our life. We perceive things, evaluate them, and act upon them, all at the same time. But there can be no theory of values. All that a philosopher can do is to tell us what value is, and how it functions in our life. He cannot possibly presume to tell us what is and what is not valuable.

There is a real difficulty at this point in Sartre's philosophy which he did not in any way solve, at least until he abandoned Existentialism. In *Being and Nothingness* he seems to be saying that we must each decide for ourselves how to live, what is good and what is bad, and that this is a purely personal decision, which no one can take on behalf of another. But there is an element in genuine evaluation which will not submit to this analysis. If, for example, a man judges sincerely that tax evasion is wrong, then in some sense he has, whether he knows it or not, judged that it is wrong in general, and he may even believe, though without saying as much, that it is wrong necessarily, or absolutely. To say that something is wrong is certainly not merely to describe it. But neither is it merely to express one's own private feeling about it. 'Wrong' *means* 'wrong in general', unless special precautions are taken to ensure that it means less than this. To attach such a meaning to the words 'right' and 'wrong' is not to be guilty of Bad Faith. It is simply to use the words in their ordinary sense.

And so Sartre has not said enough, when he insists that human beings cannot find absolute values in the world, they can only pretend to themselves to do so. He has not taken account of the facts of forming moral opinions. It is true that in one much publicized essay, frequently translated into English and, understandably, frequently taken to be the definitive statement of his moral views, he attempts a solution to the problem of how to construct an Existentialist morality. In this essay, *Existentialism is a Humanism* (1946), Sartre tries to defend Existentialism against the charge that it was a negative, gloomy, and depressing philosophy. He argues that, far from being gloomy, Existentialism is an optimistic philosophy, since it inspires people to action by showing them the extent of their freedom to action; and it also shows them that they are responsible not only for their own destinies but for other people's as well. For whatever a man chooses, he chooses for everyone and not only for himself; for the notion of choice entails the notion of a thing's being good, and 'good' means 'good for everyone'. Thus if a man chooses freedom for himself, he is thereby committed to choosing freedom for everyone.

There is a great deal that is confused and wrong-headed in this essay. It is worthy of mention for two reasons. First, it does meet the specific objection raised above, that there could be no such thing as an Existentialist morality, if all that a man must do is to evaluate the world for himself alone; but secondly, it must be mentioned simply because Sartre himself repudiated it later, and expressed a wish that it had not been published. It is easy to see that the superficially Kantian moral theory contained in the essay might seem at first attractive, and a way out of the negative conclusions of *Being and Nothingness*. But in fact, as Sartre came to see, it is quite impossible to envisage the true Existentialist man taking on responsibility for anyone's choice but his own, or adopting the Kantian view that rational beings are to be treated as ends in themselves. For, in the first place, to pretend that anything whatever is an *end in itself* cannot be anything but the 'Spirit of Seriousness' or Bad Faith of the very kind to which moral philosophers are a prey. Secondly, it is not possible to reconcile the view that other rational creatures are ends in themselves for us, or even that they should be, with the view of our relations with other people which is central to *Being and Nothingness*. No high-minded consideration of humanity as a whole could possibly operate in the face of the basic hostility and rivalry which is there said to constitute the connection between one person and another. It seems, then, that we must abandon the attempt to consider *Existentialism is a Humanism* as a proper statement of Sartre's moral philosophy or of Existentialist moral philosophy in general.

In fact it seems to be a mistake to think of Existentialism as, in its later manifestations, making any contribution to moral philosophy at all. It is essentially a philosophy which seeks to place man in his context in the world, and only incidentally does it tell us what are or ought to be the relations between one man and another in society. A moral agent, Sartre tells us at the end of *Being and Nothingness*, must realize that he himself is the source of all values. But when he realizes this, it will affect not his choice so much as his way of seeing himself in the world. Here we have once again the desire which we first encountered in Kierkegaard, to open the eyes of his readers to some new truth about themselves and the world. Sartre is missionary, but he does not think that there is anything that we ought to *do*, only that there is something new that we ought to think and feel. He says of the moral agent, 'His freedom will become conscious of itself in anguish, as the unique source of value, and as the emptiness by which the world exists.'

The moral question for each agent is therefore how he personally is going to use his freedom in reacting to and perhaps changing his environment; how much responsibility he is going to accept for the world which he comes to realize is partly his own creation. His actions will now all of them seem significant, though in a sense it will not matter very much what they are. It is possible for him to do nothing at all, and yet to be living his life free from Bad Faith, and choosing himself. But in the long run, a man is doomed to fail to achieve that which he is inevitably to aim for. We have seen already how Sartre thinks that people must evaluate things, and must propose values to themselves as ideals. But being values, they can never be realized.

Every Being-for-itself is committed, moreover, to a longing to achieve the solid existence of the In-itself. And this again is something which he cannot do. People are bound to fail. It is not possible to escape from the note of doom upon which *Being and Nothingness* ends.

Every human reality is a passion in that it projects losing itself so as to constitute the In-itself which escapes contingency by being its own foundation, the *Ens causa sui*, which religions call God. Thus the passion of man is the reverse of that of Christ, for man loses himself as man, in order that God may be born. But the idea of God is contradictory, and we lose ourselves for nothing. Man is a useless passion.

However Sartre did promise, despite the apparent hopelessness of any such undertaking, to write another book 'on an ethical plane'. And in a footnote to his discussion, in Part III of *Being and Nothingness*, concerning the doomed nature of our relations with others, he wrote: 'These considerations do not exclude the possibility of an ethics of deliverance and salvation. But this can be achieved only after a radical conversion which we cannot discuss here.' There is little doubt that the radical conversion is the conversion to Marxism, and that the book which he promised to write on an ethical plane is the *Critique of Dialectical Reason*, which was published in 1960.

A clue to the connection between this work and Sartre's earlier writings is to be found in an essay which he published in 1957 entitled *The Question of Method*. This essay was part of a collection by various authors who were examining the position of Existentialism at that time. In this essay he distinguishes between a philosophy and an ideology. Every age, he claims, has one and only one dominant philosophy, and a variety of ideologies which grow up, as it were, under its wing. Any philosopher, whether he realizes it or not, and whether he is consciously in favour of, or hostile to, the dominant philosophy of his age, will in fact write only that which can be understood as a part of this dominant philosophy. In the twentieth century, Sartre argues, the dominant philosophy is Marxism. Existentialism is an ideology conceived within its framework. The Existentialist view of the world may, he concedes, have some contribution to make to philosophy, but only in so far as it succeeds in illuminating some aspect of Marxist theory.

Marxism was strongly criticized by Sartre in an earlier essay, published in *Les Temps Modernes* in 1946, and translated into English under the title *Materialism and Revolution*. The grounds of criticism are mainly the confusion which Sartre at that time found in the concept of dialectical materialism. He interprets the theory of the dialectical nature of history as meaning that all phenomena in the world are interconnected, or, in other words, that it would be possible in principle to give an account of the world as a complete totality. But this notion, he claims, is incompatible with the idea of materialism, the elements of whose explanations must be quantitative, and therefore must be independent units, none of them influenced or changed by the existence of the others. The difficulties and inadequacies of this argument need not, happily, concern us here. The negative and critical part of the essay is the least interesting part of it. Sartre goes on to argue that, instead of embracing an essentially incoherent materialism, which is nothing but a myth, a philosopher must substitute a true and credible account of the forces of revolution, which must start with an analysis of the revolutionary mind.

There follows a description of the revolutionary worker which might have come straight from the pages of *Being and Nothingness*. The revolutionary is the man who necessarily goes beyond the situation in which he finds himself, in order to change it. He must therefore detach himself from the present and take an historical view, regarding himself as an historical agent. He sees the future as something which can become exactly as he envisages it. 'Any plan for changing the world is inseparable from a certain understanding which reveals the world from the viewpoint of the change one wishes to bring about in it.' The lack of distinction, implicit in the Existentialist writing both of Merleau-Ponty and of Sartre himself, between the cognitive and the practical is here of the greatest significance. For the revolutionary, plainly, action to change the world must have primacy over mere knowledge of it. Sartre sums up the philosopher's task in these words: 'What is needed is a philosophical theory which shows that human reality *is* action, and that action upon the universe is identical with the understanding of that universe as it is, or, in other words, that action is the unmasking of reality, and at the same time a modification of that reality.'

What is new in this essay is the insistence that the human freedom which consists in the possibility of detaching oneself from one's situation and envisaging a different future, must be essentially understood in the context of *history*; and not, now, merely the history of the individual free agent, but the history of him as a revolutionary—that is to say, as a member of a certain *class* in *society*. So, though Marxism was not yet acceptable to Sartre, it is clear that the process of conversion had begun by 1946.

By the time of the publication of *The Question of Method*, when Sartre proposed to allow Existentialism merely to contribute to the illumination of Marxism, he had gone much further, and intended to use Existentialism to revivify precisely the materialist myth which he condemned in 1947. But even this is not the most radical change from the days of *Being and Nothingness*. If we go on from the *Question of Method* to the *Critique of Dialectical Reason* itself, we see that Sartre has given up his attempt to present and prove human freedom by reference to the concrete fact that we each experience our own freedom in anguish. He has given up the presentation of the Being-for-himself as conscious of himself in the world. The anecdotes, and the characters in them whom we can recognize and with whom we identify ourselves, have gone. Even the promise to 'interiorize' Marxism, to give life to its dead bones by means of Existentialism, which might have led us to expect an analysis of the revolutionary situation from within, is broken. There are a few, but very few, examples which might be thought to attempt this, but on the whole they are very perfunctory. In general, on the contrary, the agent of change in history turns out to be, not the individual free revolutionary, but the group of which he is a member. His enemy is not, as it was before, another individual man with whom he is locked in conflict which arises out of their very nature as conscious beings. His enemy is another class in society, and the cause of his enmity is the contingent fact of the scarcity of material goods.

Yet, startling though these changes are, and difficult though it is to see anything of Existentialism in the resultant sociological analysis, which constitutes what we so far have of the *Critique of Dialectical Reason*, it is possible to understand to some extent why this had to come about. We have seen how, at the end of *Being and Nothingness*, Sartre was faced with an *impasse*. Any attempt at an account of ethics that would have any generality was to be condemned as Bad Faith. The one established fact seemed to be that values were contingent, personal, and chosen, if they were genuine, by the individual, by himself, and for himself alone. There was no method by which he could hope permanently to establish a community of ends with other human beings, since he was locked in inevitable conflict with others, and could not argue that either he or they had any *natural* rights or duties towards each other. The whole notion of natural or inalienable rights, like that of absolute values, expressed merely the 'Spirit of Seriousness', the natural wish that there were something fixed in the sea of contingency. But wishing that one had some lines of guidance in the problems of living in society, wishing that everything and everybody were not equally *de trop*, did not make it so.

There was therefore *no* rational way open for Existentialism to order life in society. The only remaining rule appeared to be that each must save himself, by choosing his own life of freedom. Just as Authenticity, for Heidegger, consisted in each man launching himself freely towards his own destiny, which was death, so Sartre's Being-for-himself would redeem himself only by knowingly making his own decisions, for himself alone. But this must have seemed inadequate to Sartre who was and is, after all, an almost wholly political man. If any *political* policy is to be judged better than another, if there is ever any aspect of society of which one is to be able to say with certainty that it is wrong and must be eliminated, then there must be found some positive answer to the

moralists' question 'How ought men to live?' The radical conversion without which Sartre had said that it was impossible to
establish a philosophy of salvation, had to be a conversion to
Marxism. For not only did Marxism present something, namely
revolution, which seemed to be good, and within our power to
bring about, but it also presented a means by which my good
could be shown to be someone else's good as well. It was only by
ceasing to consider people one by one, as individuals, and beginning to consider them as members of a class of people with an
identical approach to the world, and an identical means of connection with it, namely work, that Sartre could see a way of treating
their interests as identical. The only possible end to isolation was
the new belief that *first and foremost* men must be considered as
members of a group, because at the very beginning of society, as
an historical fact, they had formed themselves into groups precisely in order to escape from 'seriality', the new name for the
situation in which everyone is *de trop*. In the group, by its very
nature, everyone is dependent upon everyone else, and therefore
no one is dispensable. It is therefore possible to treat all men as
my brothers, and to identify my lot with theirs. The original choice
of freedom was the original and radical conversion, the formation
of the group. And thereafter every measure which is aimed towards
the preservation of the group is a further choice of freedom.

The aim of *The Critique of Dialectical Reason* is to analyse the
growth and preservation of the group, and to show what features
of human history make it necessary that society should have
developed in the way that it has. This is a far cry from the anti-
scientific passion of *Being and Nothingness*. It is impossible not
to reflect that the poor Being-for-himself, who perhaps managed to
escape the fate of being sucked back from his free projects by the
sticky adhesive mess of his Freudian past, has now been thoroughly
sucked back into the equally viscous chaos of the Marxist historical
origins of society. That he is still supposed to choose his own way
out, albeit now collectively, by looking to his now collective future,
is not very much consolation. But perhaps it is only just that
Existentialism, which, as I hope to have suggested, had its origin
firmly in the nineteenth century, having managed to escape the
domination of one of the great giants of nineteenth-century
thought, should finally succumb to the other.

7
Conclusion

WE have seen how, in *The Critique of Dialectical Reason*, Existentialism has finally succumbed to Marxism. There are practically none of its own features left. Not only does it not look like a dominant philosophy, in Sartre's words, but it hardly emerges as an ideology either. The individual has ceased to be the central figure, and has been submerged in the group. The world is no longer seen as having significance for one man; the standpoint of the author is no longer *in* the world, but above it. The goal to be aimed at is not individual but, perhaps, political freedom.

The development and self-preservation of the group may well be the proper subject-matter of history, of anthropology or of sociology, but not of philosophy. Indeed Sartre intended *The Critique of Dialectical Reason* to provide the foundation for all dialectical thinking. And, though it is far from clear exactly what is meant by this, yet he was enough of an orthodox Marxist by the time he wrote it to believe that dialectical thinking meant historical thinking of any kind. He also believed that the study of history, or the study of man, could be identified with sociology. In fact in his introduction to the *Critique*, he does not distinguish between the study of history, and the more scientific studies of anthropology and sociology. All alike are to be founded on the theoretical basis expounded in the book. The French, it may be thought, are, in their intellectual life, somewhat prone to crazes. And, having gone through a craze of phenomenology—during which, it has been pointed out, practically one hundred per cent of the new books on philosophical subjects were entitled 'The Phenomenology of such-and-such'—they have now embarked upon a craze for

Anthropology and Sociology. Sartre has been replaced as an intellectual giant by Lévi-Strauss, and Existentialism has given way before Structuralism. Here we need not pursue it.

Many writers on Existentialism see it as, above all, an exploration of human freedom, and a statement of the autonomy of the individual human being. They would therefore agree that such a philosophical tradition could not possibly assimilate sociological theories, since these are primarily concerned with people not as individuals but as essentially repeatable items in a class or other social structure. There is no sociology which is not, in intention, at least, scientific. It has often been held, moreover, that the appeal of Existentialism has been largely practical, and that people have been fascinated by it because they actually want to put its principles of individual freedom into practice in society. This seems to me more dubious. But, for example, Frederick A. Olafson, one of the most serious and perceptive writers about Existentialism, concludes his book *Principles and Persons* by saying that as long as there are any forces in society which tend to prevent people from jointly and freely participating in the direction of their own affairs, Existentialism 'under whatever name, with its insistent emphasis on the centrality within human nature of the capacity for constructing alternatives and choosing among them' ought to be read and taken seriously.

There is no doubt that in one of its aspects Existentialism did indeed have this practical effect, namely that of bringing people to think of themselves as free and autonomous in a way which they did not recognize before. Moreover, as we have seen, the Existentialist's theoretical disinclination to distinguish between knowing, feeling, and acting, in addition to the initially shocking and missionary spirit which enlivened the writings of Kierkegaard, all contributed to the view, quite properly held, that Existentialist philosophy constituted, at least in part, a practical and politically useful programme.

But though this is one aspect of the matter, there are others. Other philosophers than the Existentialists have, after all, believed in, argued for, and sought to prove the freedom of man, and his capacity to make choices, and have been more actively concerned than they to reconcile this freedom with political society. On the other hand none except Existentialists have developed the peculiar methodology, which, far more than their common subject-matter, seems to me to unite them into a recognizable 'school' of philosophy.

By the methodology of Existentialism, I mean far more than a particular philosophical style; and no discussion of it could be separated from a discussion of the subject-matter upon which it is employed. The methodology consists in a perfectly deliberate and intentional use of the *concrete* as a way of approaching the abstract, the *particular* as a way of approaching the general. I have called attention already to this feature of Existentialist philosophy. I believe it is hard to find a parallel to it in any other philosopher, or rather, that wherever one found it, one would be inclined to suggest that the philosopher who used this method was really an Existentialist. By way of conclusion, I will illustrate this salient feature a little further.

We may, for brevity, term this Existentialist characteristic the 'Concrete Imagination'. It is this which has made it possible for Existentialism to have such an immediate and also a widespread appeal; it is this which has brought Existentialist philosophy so near to literature, and, often, so far from what we may think of as academic philosophy. (The literary character of Existentialism has certainly had nothing to do with any felicity of style. On the whole academic philosophers have far surpassed Existentialists in clarity and elegance of expression.) Even the missionary spirit of Existentialism, the desire to convert the reader and change his way of life, is connected with this same Concrete Imagination. This, combined with its noticeable hostility both to science and sometimes to academic philosophy, has given Existentialism great popular appeal, and has often in the past made students of philosophy feel that if only they could include Existentialism in their syllabus, they would have something real and relevant to read, which has somehow been hidden from them by the obstinacy and pedantry of their academic teachers.

The employment of the Concrete Imagination was not, obviously, just an accidental feature of Existentialism. Kierkegaard, as we saw, actually condemned abstract thought, and identified inwardness, the aim of philosophy, with Truth-for-the-thinker, and both with concrete thought. In so far as he was concerned with morality, he absolutely rejected the Kantian idea that true morality must consist in the establishment of general absolute rules. General rules, like abstract thought itself, were death to inwardness. Even though morality must consist for a Christian in the obedience to the command of God, yet God could command what was eccentric, unique, and peculiar to the situation of the particular human being, as he commanded Abraham to do something which was directly contrary to the ordinary general rules of morality. No one who was not capable of devising his own way of life was capable, in Kierkegaard's view, of Existence. And here we may note in passing how little difference it makes to Existentialist theory whether it includes or does not include a belief in God. For in practice there is no help to be found in *believing in God*. The responsibility for the interpretation of God's will is placed squarely upon the agent; and no one else's interpretation will do. Each one, in his own particular situation, must interpret his feeling that he *must* do this or that as the command of God, if he feels that he can. Even the voice speaking to him in divine tones is obeyed only because he personally takes it for a divine voice.

When we come to those philosophers who, unlike Kierkegaard, can without reservation be termed Existentialists we see that what was a theoretical demand in Kierkegaard has become an established part of their method and of their whole way of thinking. We have insisted on the debt of the Existentialists to Husserl's phenomenology; and in many ways this is right. Neither Heidegger nor Sartre can possibly be considered without reference to Husserl. But at the same time it must be repeated that the Phenomenological Reduction was initially introduced in the interests of science, or at least in the hope that it would form the foundation of a scientific method which at last would reveal the most general and abstract truths about the world. But the *generality* of the truths to be revealed, and finally the method of Reduction itself, became, in the end, repugnant to Existentialists. If there is any respect in which Heidegger remains part of the phenomenological movement, it is a very different kind of phenomenology from Husserl's which he practises, and with a very different end in view.

Our consideration of Heidegger was, it is true, limited and confined to that part of his work which has a reasonable claim to be called Existentialist. In this part, the change from phenomenology is certainly striking. In *Mind* for 1929, Gilbert Ryle reviewed *Sein und Zeit*, and opened his review by saying that he regarded the advance in the application of the phenomenological method to be found in this book as 'an advance towards disaster'. He concluded by saying that he foresaw for phenomenology nothing but 'either self-ruinous subjectivism or . . . windy mysticism'. In the course of the review, he made an all-important distinction between the theories of Husserl and those of Heidegger which developed out of them. Husserl, he wrote, 'though he reached the point of saying that Being is nothing but . . . what consciousness has as its "accusative", had never quite emancipated himself from the Cartesian point of view that Consciousness and Being are *vis-a-vis* to one another in such a way that in studying Consciousness we are studying something on the outside of which and transcending which lies a region of absolute reality'. In this way he could keep separate the spheres of phenomenology and ontology. But Heidegger regarded this very temptation which we have—to treat Being and Consciousness as separable—as itself the first subject of analysis. He therefore set about the task of analysing the fundamental relation of consciousness to the world, the relation which creates for us a world *apparently* distinct from ourselves. 'The world that I am in in this sense', says Ryle, 'is all that it *means* to me. It is what makes me an experiencer of experiences . . . in a word, the world that I am "in" is simply the sum of what I am "about".'

We have seen that in fact Husserl went far, himself, in the direction of rejecting Cartesian dualism, and also of seeking meanings in the world which people construct for themselves. Nevertheless, his beings are still in some sense looking out upon a world which it is possible to 'put in brackets'. It is because the whole subject matter of the first part of *Sein und Zeit* is *Dasein*, conscious human beings *in the world*, that it becomes necessary for Heidegger actually to consider the world, literally, and in concrete detail. The concrete imagination, in his case, must be exercised on the very task which he has set himself, namely the analysis of the world of *Dasein*. It is impossible to speak of consciousness abstracted from its world of significance. The original statement of Brentano, that consciousness is always consciousness *of* something, has become an urgent demand that the world and its occupants should be treated together. The crucial change from phenomenology to Existentialism comes at this point.

When the meaning of the world of consciousness (the 'care' of consciousness for the world) comes to be analysed, the method is to reveal meanings in the world which, the moment we understand them, we are supposed to recognize as the meanings which we had in fact assigned to the world all along. It is a method like that of psycho-analysis. It is in fact the psycho-analysis of *things* of which Sartre spoke in *Being and Nothingness*. Thus, when Heidegger, in distinguishing inauthentic from authentic being, says of the inauthentic man that he will submit to living his life as if he were a Person-in-general, and illustrates this way of life by reference to the wearing of ready-made clothes or the using of public bus-shelters, these familiar features of our life are presented to us in a new light, and we are asked to accept them as having a significance which we did not realize before, and yet which, now that we have seen it, we cannot deny. The method of 'hermeneutic phenomenology' just is an exercise in the concrete imagination. It could not be pursued at all except in particular and concrete detail.

The Existentialist philosopher, then, must above all *describe* the world in such a way that its meanings emerge. He cannot, obviously, describe the world as a whole. He must take examples in as much detail as he can, and from these examples his intuition of significance will become clear. It is plain how close such a method is to the methods of the novelist, the short-story writer, or the serious maker of films. Earlier in the course of discussing Heidegger's belief that Being itself could be grasped in some such way as this, a comparison between him and Coleridge was quoted. It seems to me that perhaps only in Coleridge, among English writers, does one find this kind of belief that if one looks closely enough at the details of the world, one will find there, not analogies, but actual visible instances of the structure of reality. One can *read* the world, and, by looking at it in detail, one can understand its meaning. Coleridge believed, for instance, that in the whirling movement of water in a stream or rock pool one could actually see the whole principle of metamorphosis which governed change and growth throughout the universe, in the spirit of man, as well as in matter. And because this very metamorphosis is to be seen in water, as in every other aspect of nature, it is worth seeing the water in absolutely minute detail, not only for its own sake, nor for the sake of its beauty, but for what it reveals. Indeed the fascination which it exercises on the beholder is to be explained only by its *meaning*. One cannot separate the appearance from the meaning 'What a sight it is', Coleridge writes, 'to look on such a cataract. The wheels that circumvolve in it, the leaping up and plunging forward of that infinity of Pearls and Glass Bulbs, the continual change of the matter, the perpetual sameness of the form.' And again, 'Scattered Os rapidly uncoiling into serpent spirals . . . O how slow a word is rapidly to express the life and time-mocking Motion of that change, always Os before, always spirals, coiling, uncoiling *being*.' Over and over again, in all sorts of contexts, Coleridge expressed this fascination with the bubbling of water. 'The moon', he later wrote, 'thinned and thinned and thinned till *once* it became a star, at its vanishing . . . but immediately after sent up a *throb* of light in its former shape and dimension, and so for several seconds it throbbed and heaved, a soft boiling up or restlessness of a fluid in carrying.' And, most explicitly, of a stream again, in a famous passage he wrote of 'the white eddy-rose that blossom'd up against the stream in the scollop, by fits and starts, obstinate in resurrection . . . it *is the life* that we live'. It is wrong in this context to speak of metaphor. The connection between the observable natural phenomenon, the stream or the moon, and its meaning is too close to be thought of in these terms. One may speak, perhaps, of the water or the moon as a symbol, but only in the sense in which the written or spoken word is a symbol. We have become so much accustomed to the word's meaning what it does, that normally we simply understand it as though it were transparent. So it is with these natural phenomena with which Coleridge was obsessed in his search for meanings.

Let us now compare this with what Sartre says about the viscous, towards the end of *Being and Nothingness*. We have already seen how he comes to regard the viscous as the Anti-value, evoking a response of horror and disgust from anyone who contemplates it, as that feature of the world most to be dreaded. He insists that one does not have to *learn* to regard the viscous in this way. 'Man, being transcendence, establishes the meaningful by his very coming into the world.' So things have meanings for us necessarily, and their meanings may be analysed and revealed, but they cannot be thought of as accidental, neither can one consider the physical properties of material objects without thereby considering them as meaningful. We treat the physical qualities which things have, and which are available to us, as clues to the nature of being itself. 'In each apprehension of a quality, there is . . . a metaphysical effort to escape from our condition so as to pierce through the shell of nothingness about the "there is", and to penetrate to the pure In-itself.' The psycho-analysis of things ought to disclose precisely the metaphysical purport of visible and tangible properties. The more minutely, therefore, and the more accurately the visible and tangible properties of things are described, the more possible it will be to see what they mean, and in what way they 'reveal being'.

Sartre is thus arguing for just the kind of description which Coleridge practised in his Notebooks. And he himself, as we have seen, goes on in the same section of *Being and Nothingness* to describe the viscous as an example of the kind of description which the psycho-analysis of things ought to undertake.

The honey which slides off my spoon onto the honey in the jar first sculptures the surface by fastening itself on it in relief, and its fusion with the whole is presented as a gradual sinking, a collapse which appears both as a deflation . . . and as display, like the flattening out of the full breasts of a woman who is lying on her back. . . . The slowness of the disappearance of the viscous drop in the bosom of the whole is grasped first in *softness* which is like a slowed-down annihilation and seems to be playing for time; but this softness lasts up to the end. The drop is *sucked into* the body of the viscous substance. . . . The mode of being [of the viscous] is neither the reassuring inertia of the solid nor a dynamism like that of water, which is exhausted in fleeing from me. It is a soft yielding *action*, a moist and feminine sucking, it lives obscurely under my fingers, and I sense it like a dizziness; it draws me to it as the bottom of a precipice might draw me. There is a tactile fascination in the viscous.[1]

All these, and others, are features of the viscous which we may simply notice, if we keep our eyes open, and if we also honestly consider our own feelings and attitudes. And *if* we do this, then the meaning of viscosity will be revealed. We shall understand it, as our attitude to it shows that in a way we have already understood it, as speaking directly to us of the threat which is built into the very structure of the world, that we might be taken over, annihilated, and our consciousness sucked away from us. We hate the viscous because of our precarious position, as conscious beings, in an alien world.

The Cartesian distinction between mind and body has indeed been left behind by the Existentialists. No one who was, as they were, concerned with *Dasein*, with human beings *in the world*, could possibly adopt so naively dualistic a view of the world as Descartes did. As we have seen, Husserl's greatest innovations led

[1] op. cit., pt. iv, ch. 2, sec. 3.

him away from Cartesianism, and the process was completed by the Existentialists. But all the same, *res extensa*, Beings-in-themselves, remain to some extent recalcitrant. We may, in a sense, construct our own world; we may see objects primarily as tools for our own use; we may ascribe meanings to things; but all the same there remains 'the coefficient of adversity'. Things are capable of frustrating us. There is an inescapable *fact* about the world, which is that Beings-for-themselves are separate from the rest of the world; and part of what they understand, in understanding the gap between themselves and the things around them, is that the world is *not* wholly manageable, and might in the end turn and submerge them.

This is the truth which Sartre seeks to expose by the Concrete Imagination. No account of Existentialism which failed to emphasize this imaginative and descriptive aspect could possibly be complete. The popular belief that Existentialism was engaged with real things, with actual life and not with 'mere words' like Anglo-Saxon philosophy, stems indeed from this source.

This may have been the strength of the Existentialist movement, which has certainly sometimes seemed a desirable refuge from the aridities of other philosophy. But it has, I believe, also been its downfall. There is no real possibility of *argument* with the deliverances of the concrete imagination. If I see significance in some feature of the world around me, I am at liberty to say so. If I am a poet or a painter or a photographer or film maker, then my vision of the world can be understood, perhaps shared, and may even be analysed, but argument need not come into the matter. But philosophy without arguments is not possible, in the long run. We may be struck by the image of the man listening at the keyhole and caught in the act; we may be enlightened by it. But we cannot be expected to accept a whole theory of interpersonal relations, and therefore of morality, on the basis of this picture. The fact is that in philosophy we wish to theorize about the world. We do not wish merely to describe it, or have it described, even if, like Heidegger, the philosopher offers us a whole new vocabulary of description. It is, obviously, unwise to predict the future course of the history of philosophy, but it is perhaps safe to say that, at least for the time being, Existentialism, however attractive its doctrines of individual freedom may be, has come to an end as a philosophical movement; and this is partly because its methods were becoming less and less philosophical, not just as a matter of fact, but as a matter of policy. The Existentialists have given us many particular insights, especially in their discussions of persons, and of perception, but, if philosophy is to continue to exist, then it is necessary to reject the subjective anti-scientific dogmatism of their attempt to reveal the ultimate meaning of Existence.

Select Bibliography

I SELECTION OF TEXTS IN ENGLISH TRANSLATION

Kierkegaard
Concluding Unscientific Postscript (1846), translated by D. F. Swenson and W. Lowrie (Princeton, 1941).

Nietzsche
The Philosophy of Nietzsche (including *Thus Spake Zarathustra* (1883), *Beyond Good and Evil* (1886), *The Genealogy of Morals* (1887), and *The Birth of Tragedy* (1872), translated by O. Levy (New York, 1937).
The Philosophy of Nietzsche (a selection of the above translation), edited with an introduction by G. Clive (New York, 1965).
Thus Spake Zarathustra, translated by A. Tille (London, 1958).
The Will to Power (1895), translated by W. Kaufmann and R. J. Hollingdale, edited by W. Kaufmann (London, 1968).

Husserl
Ideas (1913), translated by W. R. Boyce Gibson (London, 1931).
The Idea of Phenomenology (1907), translated by W. P. Alston and G. Nakhnikian (The Hague, 1964).
Cartesian Meditations (1931), translated by D. Cairns (The Hague, 1960).
'Phenomenology', article in *Encyclopaedia Britannica* (14th edn., 1927).
The Paris Lectures (1929), translated by P. Koestenbaum (The Hague, 1964).

Heidegger
Being and Time (1927), translated by J. Macquarrie and E. Robinson (London, 1967).
Existence and Being, four essays translated with an introduction by W. Brock (London, 1949).

Merleau-Ponty

The Structure of Behaviour (1942), translated by A. Fisher (Boston, 1963).

The Phenomenology of Perception (1945), translated by C. Smith (London, 1962).

Sartre

Imagination (1936), translated by F. Williams (Michigan, 1962).

Sketch of a Theory of the Emotions (1939), translated by P. Mairet (London, 1962).

The Psychology of the Imagination (1940), translated by B. Frechtman (London, 1949).

Being and Nothingness (1943), translated by Hazel Barnes (London, 1957).

Saint Genet (1952), translated by B. Frechtman (London, 1964).

Nausea (1938), translated by L. Alexander (London, 1962).

Existentialism and Humanism (1946), translated by P. Mairet (London, 1948).

II SELECTED STUDIES, DISCUSSIONS AND COLLECTED ESSAYS

Spiegelberg, H., *The Phenomenological Movement* (The Hague, 1965).

Lowrie, W., *A Short Life of Kierkegaard* (London, 1943).

Danto, A. C., *Nietzsche as Philosopher* (New York, 1965).

Hollingdale, R., *Nietzsche, The Man and his Philosophy* (London, 1964).

Olafson, F. A., *Principles and Persons: An Ethical Interpretation of Existentialism* (Baltimore, Md., 1967).

Kockelman, J. D., *A First Introduction to Husserl's Phenomenology* (Pittsburgh, 1967).

— *Husserl's Phenomenological Psychology* (Pittsburgh, 1967).

Sokolowski, R., 'The Formation of Husserl's Concept of Constitution', *Phaenomenologica*, 18 (1964).

Grene, Marjorie, *Martin Heidegger* (London, 1957).

Langan, T., *The Meaning of Heidegger* (London, 1959).

Richardson, W. J., 'Heidegger: Through Phenomenology to Thought', *Phaenomenologica*, 13 (1963).

Kwant, R. C., *From Phenomenology to Metaphysics*, an inquiry into the last period of Merleau-Ponty's philosophical life (Pittsburgh, 1966).

Rabil, A., *Merleau-Ponty: Existentialist of the Social World* (New York, 1967).

Murdoch, Iris, *Sartre, Romantic Rationalist* (Cambridge, 1953).

Warnock, Mary, *The Philosophy of Sartre* (London, 1965).

Manser, A., *Sartre* (London, 1966).

Laing, R. D., and Cooper, D. G., *Reason and Violence* (London, 1964).

Lee, E. N., and Mandelbaum, M., (eds.), *Phenomenology and Existentialism*, a collection of essays (Baltimore, Md., 1967).

Lawrence, N., and O'Connor, D. (eds.), *Readings in Existential Phenomenology* (Englewood Cliffs, N. J., 1967).

Index

145

OXFORD

OPUS

General Editors
Keith Thomas
Alan Ryan
Walter Bodmer

OPUS books provide concise, original, and authoritative introductions to a wide range of subjects in the humanities and sciences. They are written by experts for the general reader as well as for students.

Most of the titles listed below are only available in paperback editions; some, however, are available in both hardback and paperback, and a few in hardback only. Further details of OPUS books, and complete lists of Oxford Paperbacks, including The World's Classics, Twentieth-Century Classics, Past Masters, Oxford Authors, Oxford Shakespeare, and Oxford Paperback Reference, as well as OPUS, is available from the General Publicity Department, Oxford University Press, Walton Street, Oxford OX2 6DP.

In the USA, complete lists are available from the Paperbacks Marketing Manager, Oxford University Press, 200 Madison Avenue, New York, NY 10016.

Architecture

The Shapes of Structure
Heather Martienssen

Business

The Way People Work
Job Satisfaction and the Challenge of Change
Christine Howarth

Economics

The Economics of Money
A. C. L. Day

History

The Industrial Revolution, 1760–1830
T. S. Ashton

Literature

The Modern American Novel
Malcolm Bradbury

This Stage-Play World
English Literature and its Background, 1580–1625
Julia Briggs

Medieval Writers and their Work
English Literature and its Background, 1100–1500
J. A. Burrow

Romantics, Rebels and Reactionaries
English Literature and its Background, 1760–1830
Marilyn Butler

Ancient Greek Literature
Kenneth Dover and others

British Theatre since 1955
Ronald Hayman

Modern English Literature
W. W. Robson

Mathematics

What is Mathematical Logic?
J. N. Crossley and others

Medical Sciences

What is Psychotherapy?
Sidney Bloch

The Standing of Psychoanalysis
B. A. Farrell

Man Against Disease
Preventative Medicine
J. A. Muir Gray

Philosophy

Aristotle the Philosopher
J. L. Arkrill

The Philosophy of Aristotle
D. J. Allan

Character

The Philosophy of Mind
Colin McGinn

Moral Philosophy
D. D. Raphael

The Problems of Philosophy
Bertrand Russell

Structuralism and Since
From Lévi-Strauss to Derrida
Edited by John Sturrock

Free Will and Responsibility
Jennifer Trusted

Ethics since 1900
Mary Warnock

Existentialism
Mary Warnock